ADVENTURES ON TWO WHEELS IN THE BEAUTIFUL VALE OF STRATHMORE

by John Palfreyman

The Palfreyman Press
The Neuk, Caddam Road, Coupar Angus

© John Palfreyman 2013

First edition 2013

ISBN:

Printed by Winter & Simpson, Dundee

Design & production: Arc Visual Communications Ltd

The photographs were taken by the author except where stated otherwise.
The cartoons were kindly provided by illustrator Scoular Anderson.

Acknowledgements – the author would like to thank local historian and author Margaret Laing for writing the sections on Strathmore and Coupar Angus, David Bradley for his constant IT support, Scoular Anderson for his cartoons, the members of Forward Coupar Angus and other community groups in the town for their enthusiasm and encouragement, Val Kidd for proof reading the text, Anne for introducing him to cycle touring, his daughters for their encouragement (and supplying an excellent pair of cycling gloves that kept him going through the cold days) and Wendy, for putting up with a certain unsociable degree of single mindedness from time to time.

Thanks are also due to Forward Coupar Angus, Perth & Kinross Council and Tayside & Central Scotland Transport Partnership (Tactran) for their co-funding contributions which have enabled publication of this guide.

Cover image: Looking towards the Sidlaw Hills from the road between Coupar Angus and Meigle.

While every effort has been made to ensure the accuracy of the information provided in this guidebook, things do change. For up to date details on the various tearooms, restaurants and inns, the reader is guided to the websites listed. Although it is not expected that the actual roads for the routes in this book will change, their status might. For example, some roads may be designated 'Green Routes'.

Contents

Introduction   2
The Vale of Strathmore   4
The Town of Coupar Angus   9
Coupar Angus as a Centre for Cycle Touring   14
Safety on your Bike   17
Types of Bike and Bike Accessories   18

The ROUTES   20
The Routes in Detail   26
        1   Le Tour de Coupar Angus   26
        2   Over the Sidlaws   28
        3   MacBeth's Castle and Dunsinane Hill   29
        4   St Martins and Waulkmill   31
        5   Cargill and the Banks of the Tay   33
        6   Stewart Tower Tour   34
        7   The Five Lochs Tour   36
        8   The Roman Camp   38
        9   Coupar Angus to Dunkeld   40
       10   Via Kirkmichael to Pitlochry   42
       11   The Drimmie Loop   44
       12   Into the Mountains   46
       13   The High Mountains   48
       14   To the Lovely Loch of Lintrathen   50
       15   Around the Loch of Lintrathen   52
       16   Kirriemuir and Peter Pan   54
       17   The Stones Tour   56
       18   Meigle and Newtyle   58
       19   Newtyle and Lundie   60
       20   Le Tour de Dundee   62
       21   Through Angus and the Mearns   64
       22   Abernyte Tour   66
       23   Sidlaw Foothills   67
       24   Low Level (Flat) Route   68
       25   Kitty Swanson's Bridge   69
       26   Stormont Loch and the Gull Colony   70
Tearooms, and Sources of Refreshment on the Cycle Routes   72
Future Publications by the Author   76
How to use the Map   78
Map of the area   Inside back cover

Introduction

The ancient small town of Coupar Angus sits near the heart of the richly fertile valley of Strathmore in the east of Scotland. Strathmore stretches from the A9 in the south west to Brechin in the north east. It is bounded, and sheltered, by the Grampian Mountains to the north and west and by the Sidlaw Hills in to the south. The largest river in the area is the Tay and some of its major tributaries, notably the Isla, are very much part of the vale's scenery. Strathmore is rather unusual in Scotland with its rich mix of rivers, small lochs, mountains, hills and pretty villages. In summer, the area is gloriously green with purple hills to the north. As the seasons change, the colours in the landscape develop, transforming the views every day. We see the rich autumnal browns and reds most notably in the famous Beech Hedge at Meikleour. In winter, the low sun highlights the dramatic hills and valleys around Strathmore and, with a coating of snow as backdrop, an altogether different and harsher beauty is revealed. In spring, a sparkling green develops and the snowdrops, primroses and bluebells soften the landscape again.

The area is rich in history with many standing stones and you can visit a world famous museum of Pictish stones in the village of Meigle just a few miles from Coupar Angus. This museum displays many examples of interesting, yet enigmatic, Pictish art. The stunning and dramatic Glamis Castle is only a 12 mile cycle ride from Coupar Angus and Macbeth's ruined castle of Dunsinane, perched high on the Sidlaw Hills, is even closer. Going further back in time, there are the remains of a 1st century Roman occupation with the Fort at Inchtuthill on the banks of the Tay near Spittalfield, and more Roman forts at Cargill, Blacks Hill, Cardean and Campmuir. What may well be Scotland's oldest ancient monument, the cursus called the Cleaven Dyke, runs north of Meikleour and is clearly visible from the nearby A93. All of these places, and more, are within easy reach by bike from Coupar Angus. What is more, the area is not densely populated so the roads are mostly quiet with lots of opportunities to stop and admire, and photograph, the stunning views.

The cycle routes in this book can be divided into two broad categories. The routes in the Vale of Strathmore are generally fairly flat. There are hills, but these are never long enough to be overpowering for the average cyclist. Then there are the routes to the north and south of the Vale, which include longer and steeper climbs. The climbs to the south, in and over the Sidlaw Hills, tend to be steep but relatively short. The climbs to the north, notably those on the routes up Glen Shee north of Blairgowrie, can be very challenging.

Throughout this guide every effort has been made to keep off the main A roads and, as Strathmore abounds with B roads and minor roads, normally this is possible. However, there are places where the A road is the only option. For example, there is only one road up Glen Shee and it is an A road (the A93). Likewise the road from Bridge of Cally to Pitlochry is an A road (the A924) and although part of the road can be avoided, this can only be achieved by more cycling on a different A road. One or two of the routes run along the main road to the north in Scotland, the A9, but this road has a very good cycle route alongside it all the way.

Distances are given for all the cycle routes in this book and approximate times for a reasonably fit cyclist, and times should be adjusted to allow for stops as appropriate. Wherever possible the guide gives information about tearooms, pubs, tourist attractions, especially good views, and so on. Opening times are correct at the time of going to press but, of course, these may change. Most of the routes have at least one possible refreshment stop but some of the shorter ones, for example the routes to the Cargill loop, are refreshment free. However Strathmore abounds with great places for picnics and there is always the 'Y' Community Café or the Red House in Coupar Angus as places to start or finish your cycle ride.

Have fun pedalling!

The Centre of Coupar Angus

The Vale of Strathmore

Looking to the West across Strathmore

In 1885, the Rev McPherson wrote 'Nature has been particularly favourable to the inhabitants of East Perthshire for they live in the most magnificent valley that Great Britain contains'. Even today, nothing has changed regarding this statement and those who know the Vale of Strathmore would not argue with this gentleman, for without doubt it is one of the most beautiful areas of Scotland.

Strathmore in its entirety stretches from Aberfoyle to Stonehaven but the Strath' that we are concerned with runs from Methven to Brechin. Coupar Angus is particularly fortunate as it is surrounded, not only by outstanding countryside, but by several beautiful small communities, towns and villages such as Bendochy, Kettins, Blairgowrie, Meigle, Alyth, Kirriemuir, Glamis and Forfar. The ancient Abbey town of Coupar Angus lies at the very centre of this beautiful area, but then the Cistercian Monks of the twelfth century chose with great care where to build their Abbeys, which were akin to small villages with their church at the heart of the community. The Abbey would have had a Storehouse, Kitchens, Refectory, Guest House, Abbot's House, Monks' Infirmary, Lay Brothers Infirmary and a Monks' Dormitory. There would also have been workshops and accommodation for the tradesmen, essential to supply the monks' every need.

But what of the people who lived in Strathmore in ancient times, people who have left traces for us to follow and to wonder and speculate about. With Coupar Angus as our central point, we travel westwards to the nearby Meikleour Woods and their Cleaven Dyke. Until recent times, the Cleaven Dyke was thought to be of Roman origin but excavations over the years have proved that it pre-dates Roman occupation by thousands of years. Who were those ancient people who constructed it? How and why was it built? How long did it take to build this dyke, which is now one of the most ancient and important monuments in Western Europe?

The Amazing Meikleour Beech Hedge

Few people know of the Cleaven Dyke, which must be one of Strathmore's best kept secrets, but the Beech Hedge of Meikleour is a very different matter. Planted in 1746, it was once considered to be one of the seven wonders of the arboreal world and is still spectacular, attracting visitors from all over the globe. Close by the hedge, on the road to Kinclaven, is the ruin of the ancient Kinclaven Castle. The castle ruin is on private land so permission to view must be obtained. It stands on high ground overlooking the river Tay where it is joined by the river Isla. The view from the castle is superb!

To the east of Coupar Angus is Kettins and the Hallyburton Estate, where a 'souterrain' has survived, in excellent condition, for thousands of years. It is considered to be, perhaps, the finest in Scotland and again is on private land. A souterrain is a tunnel-like underground structure of several interconnected passage ways which was used in Roman times and possibly earlier, when danger threatened. It acted as a refuge for the people of the time along with their animals and their grain and food. Once inside the souterrain, the people could cover over the entrance in a clever way which left no trace.

Kettins is a village closely connected to Hallyburton Estate. Like in other areas of Strathmore, the rise of the linen industry in the eighteenth century gave the natives of Kettins a much needed financial boost. In 1793, it was recorded that there were one hundred looms in the parish. From Kettins you can journey on, through splendid farm-land, to Meigle, and its collection of more than twenty Pictish stones which are on display in the former village school, now a small museum. There have been claims that Meigle is the oldest village in Scotland.

The Meigle Churchyard

Craighall in the Gorge of the Ericht

Whether this is true or not is debatable as very few old documents regarding the village are available. What is beyond dispute however, is that Meigle holds many mysteries regarding its stones. At the entrance to Meigle House there is an interesting building, now in danger of collapse, which may have been built from Coupar Angus Abbey stone.

In the kirkyard there is a stone which is believed to depict Queen Guinevere, wife of King Arthur of Round Table fame, being attacked by wild beasts. Some academics however, think the stone is of Daniel in the lion's den. Arthurian legends abound! Is it possible that he, and his Knights of the Round Table, sojourned in the Meigle area? Here again a mystery lies in the name Arthurstone, which dates back to the twelfth century and the former Cistercian Abbey. It was one of the Abbey estates. Queen Guinevere, it is said, was imprisoned in the hill fort at Alyth before being torn to pieces by dogs because of her act of unfaithfulness! Could there be any truth in these tales or must they too remain mysteries of the past?

Were the tales of the Knights of the Round Table purely myth and legend? Some certainly think so but how did these stories come about in a part of Scotland so very far from Arthur's castle in the south of England. On the road to Blairgowrie from Coupar Angus is Bendochy, a small community which, in former times, was closely connected with the Abbey at Coupar Angus. The Abbot had most certainly a house at Knowehead and historians believe the first settlement of monks was at Bendochy, which would have been a more secure and more easily defended position against the predators of the time, while the Abbey was under construction. In more recent times at Bendochy, a large slab, believed to have been a Druidic Altar, was blown up to clear the land for crops. There were also two souterrains but no trace of them remains.

Blairgowrie's most distinctive land-mark is its former Hill Kirk standing against the skyline from its superb position above the town. It is the third church to have been built on the site but sadly it is no longer a church and now belongs to the local amateur dramatic society. Its kirkyard is full of history in its ancient head-stones which are now obscured by the neglect of years. The earliest settlement in Blairgowrie was clustered around the fortified dwelling of Newton, now the residence of the Macpherson family and known as Newton Castle.

Blairgowrie was firstly a market town, and it was the river Ericht that brought prosperity and expansion in the early nineteenth century, when mills were built along its banks. Fifteen mills were built along each side of the river, all eventually servicing the jute industry. There was also a granary and some of its remaining buildings are now restaurants. Other smaller buildings are used by a chiropractor, a chiropodist and a beautician. As the textile industry declined in the late nineteenth and early twentieth centuries, the wealth the mills had created was replaced by the soft-fruit industry. Blairgowrie became known as the 'Berry Capital of the World'!

Hundreds of people descended on the town every summer, for very many decades, to harvest the fruit, as did most of the local children, who managed to earn enough from picking fruit to kit themselves out for school after their working holiday. Times change but berries are still grown in the Blairgowrie area, but now they are cultivated in plastic tunnels, with pickers from all around the world harvesting the fruit.

Blairgowrie's Wellmeadow is the part of the town where things happen. At one time the Wellmeadow was a boggy area where the drovers, on their way to the markets at Falkirk and Crieff, tethered their cattle for the night. This delightful square which contains the town's war memorial, is where markets are held as well as all kinds of entertainment. It is also a very pleasant place for people to sit and admire the flowers and hanging baskets or just watch the world go by.

On the road from Blairgowrie to Kirriemuir is Alyth, with its splendid golf courses. Alyth also produced jute and at one time had an Industrial School which became an auction sale room. This has been converted into attractive housing. There are some very charming old areas in the town. Over the River Isla, running through the town centre, is an old bridge which some say was used by the Cistercians on their way to their valuable flocks of sheep in the hills above the town. Aerial photography has revealed a very interesting archaeological landscape all around Alyth and the surrounding golf courses. There are some remains of the former parish church in the form of arches, officially known as the south aisle arcade. Like most small towns, Alyth has lost many of its shops but still remains a vibrant, attractive little place which has become popular with commuters.

Nearby, and tucked away at the edge of Strathmore, is Kirriemuir, known as Kirrie by the locals and affectionately referred to as the 'wee red toon' by its most famous son Sir J M Barrie, best known for his book and play, Peter Pan. You can visit Barrie's birthplace complete with the original Wendy House. There are many interesting shops in the cobbled lanes like Cumberland Close dedicated to other famous Kirriemarians such as Sir Hugh Munro, who listed all Scottish mountains over 3000 ft. Kirriemuir had a thriving home industry in coarse linen. Many of the red stone houses still retain their little windows where the loom would have been placed. Barrie gifted the town a cricket pavilion and the Camera Obscura at Northmuir, which is a unique way of surveying the countryside, with views stretching to the top of the Angus Glens.

Peter Pan looks over Kirriemuir

Balintore Castle

The Kirriemuir 'Den' which is a natural amphitheatre is a very beautiful place with paths leading all around it and the Gairie Burn running through it. It is sheltered from the wind and is a most pleasant place. At one time it was a popular venue for 'Sunday School Picnics'. The old fashioned street names such as 'Narrow Roods' and 'Upper Roods' still remain, for visitors to wonder about. Kirriemuir is surrounded by large country estates and Airlie Castle is close by. In the past during the shooting season the economy was boosted with orders to the local fish shop and licensed grocers in the town. On a visit to Kirriemuir in the 1950s, enquiring at the fish shop if they had prawns, the customer was told that they only had them when the 'gentry' were in the area!

Strathmore has a very great deal to offer the visitor for it is steeped in history. The ancient settlers have left an abundance of clues for us to explore tucked away in its beautiful countryside.

The Town of Coupar Angus

Central Coupar Angus

The small town of Coupar Angus has its beginnings in the twelfth century when it gradually grew around the wealthiest and most powerful Cistercian Abbey in Scotland dating from 1161, when Malcolm IV of Scotland brought monks to the area. Malcolm's generous donations of land encouraged other land-owners to follow his example. It was also believed, that being generous to the Cistercians would help reserve a place in heaven when they died.

At this period in Scotland the land was rough and boggy and covered with broom. The Cistercian monks however, were superb agriculturalists and we can see, in looking around us every day, their inheritance in the superb agricultural land all around Coupar Angus. They were given so many gifts of land that they could not work it all themselves so they rented it out to tenant farmers and carefully supervised how it was farmed. The Cistercians were the first to introduce 'leases' and the conditions had to be carefully adhered to. They stipulated which crops each tenant-farmer would grow and the number and type of livestock they would keep. The rents for the land were paid in produce such as butter, cereals, eggs, chickens and naturally these perishable items could not all be consumed by the monks and their laymen, so markets were introduced to dispose of the surplus. These markets were our first shops!

Over the years people began to settle around the Abbey for the work and the protection it afforded them. Gradually the Abbey grew in size, wealth and strength. These were turbulent times in Scotland and in 1296, the Scottish Wars of Independence began. This was to be a difficult time for the monks. King Edward, known as the Hammer of the Scots, visited the Abbey and removed much of its furnishings, silver and jewels, which were sold to finance his daughter, the Lady Elizabeth's journey to Holland where she was to be married. He also visited Kinclaven Castle where his troops carried out a great deal of damage, not only to it but to the land and crops all around. When he arrived in Scone, the Stone of Destiny was removed from there and taken to London. William Wallace also visited the Abbey of Coupar, but when the Monks heard of his imminent arrival, they fled!

The Toll Booth

The Remains of the Abbey

Over the centuries there were many visitors, but not all were predators as the Abbey was popular with the 'Royals' of the time, who regularly stayed over-night on their journeys to Scone and beyond. The Abbey was also used by them as a hunting lodge. No one, no matter how humble, was ever turned away. As time passed, the Power of Rome was not held in such awe by many Scots. Many of the monks had become corrupt and lazy. There were teenage bishops and priests who could neither read nor write. By the time Mary Queen of Scots arrived for a visit in 1562, the twentieth year of her reign, the Abbey was in a very run down state, which shocked her. The Scottish people had become dis-enchanted with Roman Catholicism and change was looming.

John Knox, an extreme Calvinist, began the work of founding a National Church which would not resemble the Roman Catholic Church. The buildings of this National Church would be dreary, somber places with nothing of beauty. Even the celebration of Christmas was abolished at this time for being too frivolous, and would remain a working day to many, until after World War II. Roman Catholicism was made illegal and would remain so until the nineteenth century.

After this period - the Reformation of the late sixteenth century - the Abbey, which had been neglected for centuries, was used as a 'quarry' by the locals. In 1859 the last arch of the former abbey was demolished to provide building material for the present-day Abbey Church. No doubt those responsible at that time thought they were being economical in using the stones. Regrettably, not much of what was then considered a 'worthless ruin' is left for us to admire.

Only a very small fragment of the Abbey's Gatehouse is left standing, which has undergone conservation work by Perth & Kinross Heritage Trust. Many older Coupar Angus properties are built of abbey stone and at one time, ornate and carved stones could be identified all around the town. Time and weather have, however, taken their toll on these interesting artefacts.

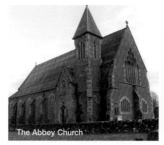
The Abbey Church

There is great speculation as to the extent of the Abbey, which would have resembled a small village. Many people wonder where the boundary walls and Abbey fish-ponds were located. Some say that in the Abbey Gardens area, traces of fish-ponds from Abbey times were uncovered when the houses were constructed. Again we wonder where would the Guest House have stood? Could the Strathmore or White House Hotel have been built on the site? It is known that this old former Hotel has a very unusual basement area, which was perhaps at one time linked to the Abbey.

Coupar Angus was once known as the 'Jewel of Strathmore' and this has been reinstated on the new signs you see when entering the town. There are still quite a number of little gems, and in order to view them, you have to leave what is now the main street through the town, and explore the little back streets of the older part. Nowadays the town centre is the area around the current Market Cross. It is an open area with the imposing former Royal Hotel.

This hotel has a long and interesting history and was once called the Defiance Inn, after the stagecoach which passed through the town on its way to Aberdeen. The hotel was re-named the 'Royal' in 1878, to mark Queen Victoria's Jubilee. Stories abound about the Queen's overnight stay in the hotel in 1844, when, it is said, one of the carriage horses suffered a heart attack and died. This caused so much damage to the carriage that the Royal Party had no option but to stay overnight in the hotel. A painting executed after the event shows her carriage and the horses being changed, while an enthusiastic crowd of local people and dignitaries look on.

An official account of the visit however, is very different, for it states that Queen Victoria did not even alight from her carriage and greeted the officials of the day through her carriage window.

After the horses were changed in Coupar Angus, the Royal Party journeyed on through Meikleour to Dunkeld, where they stopped for refreshments at the Duke of Atholl's Arms, now the Atholl Arms Hotel. The Royal Party was heading for Blair Castle, not Balmoral as the local story suggests.

How can a tale like this originate and be believed for so many years? It is thought that a teacher had told her pupils the story. One elderly man, when informed that according to the Queen's diaries, she had never stayed in the hotel, said "Where did you get that from?" and "Her diaries are wrong, I was told at school that she stayed at the hotel – so she stayed at the hotel!"*

Old Coupar Angus

Adverts for Cycles
(courtesy of Coupar Angus Heritage Centre)

The High Street of Coupar Angus is claimed to be the shortest High Street in the country. George Square (in Abbey times known as the Timber Market) leads to Gray Street – Calton Street – Hay Street – Reid's Close – Athole Street and Causewayend, where buildings of interest, little gems, are tucked away. When the railway reached Coupar Angus in the mid-nineteenth century, it brought much needed fuel, in the form of coal, to the town. The railway also brought prosperity. A number of jute factories sprang up, which employed a large workforce. All kinds of agricultural produce, including potatoes, could now be sent by rail to markets all over the country, which before the railways, were just too far away.

---

*To this day whether or not Queen Victoria visited Coupar Angus is disputed and there are many learned articles which suggest that she did. It is likely that we will never know the true story.

This was a boom-time for Coupar Angus. A cattle market thrived along with malt barns. The railway junction became one of the busiest in Scotland. In this prosperous Victorian era, the town grew rapidly and many splendid dwellings were built and new roads constructed around the perimeter of the old town.

Until the boundaries were changed in the late nineteenth century, the part of the town on the eastern side of the Coupar Burn was in the county of Angus, hence the original name of 'Cupar Angus'. At this time the spelling was changed to 'Coupar' to avoid confusion with Cupar in Fife.

The Steeple, known over time as the Tolbooth, the Clockhouse, and the Townhouse, was built in 1762 by public subscription and has had many uses. By 1876 it was in a poor state but on a visit to his native town, Thomas Lowe of Winnipeg gave £100 (quite a sum at that time) to have the steeple repaired. Then again in 1912, he had the clock-face replaced along with all the rotten wood. By the late twentieth century it underwent massive repairs and is now a 'B' Listed Building. The townsfolk of Coupar Angus were very public spirited and their early Communion Silver, Provost's Chain of Office, and even the current Town Hall were all paid for by public subscription, quite exceptional for a small town.

Yes, the small town of Coupar Angus is certainly worth a visit! Explore its narrow streets and look for its interesting buildings. It is a really enjoyable exercise to try to unravel the mysteries of this little abbey town.

The Red House Hotel Coupar Angus

Coupar Angus as a Centre for Cycle Touring

At first glance it may not be obvious why Coupar Angus is the ideal base for touring the Vale of Strathmore. Meigle, a few miles to the east, might seem a little more central and Blairgowrie, a few miles to the north, has more facilities. However, a quick look at OS Map Number 53 shows the pre-eminence of Coupar Angus. Specifically it sits at the centre of a circle of 8 roads radiating from the town. Starting from the south east and going clockwise, these are as follows:

1   The A923 main road to Dundee which leaves Coupar Angus from the relief road, past the old Tolbooth and the remains of the town's Cistercian Abbey, climbs over the Sidlaws at Tullybaccart then descends gradually to Barnhill, Muirhead, Dundee and the Tay Estuary. This is a busy, winding road and the routes in this book avoid the south bound A923 as much as possible.

2   Moving through 45° we come to a minor road which leaves the A923 almost immediately after the Tolbooth and heads south to Campmuir. This road opens into a rich network of minor roads on the north side of the Sidlaws, allowing access to such pretty villages as Abernyte, Collace and Kinrossie. The area includes Dunsinane Fort made famous by Shakespeare as the home of the Thane of Glamis, MacBeth.

3   Next is the A94 to Perth. Many of our routes cross this road and one or two follow it from Coupar Angus as far as Woodside. On the north side of the road there is a cyclable footpath in this direction. Once you get to Woodside, there is an almost parallel side road which follows the A94 or you can pick up another one once you get to neighbouring Burrelton. There is a 20 mile an hour speed limit in Burrelton, so it is safe to cycle here.

4   Our next route out of Coupar Angus needs a short ride up the A923 in a northerly direction towards Blairgowrie. Just a couple of hundred yards from the roundabout on the bypass there is a sign to the Cemetery and you follow this road, Bogside Road, to its termination at a T junction. Here you turn left then almost immediately right on to Caddam Road into another set of minor roads which eventually reach Meikleour and on to Dunkeld on the River Tay.

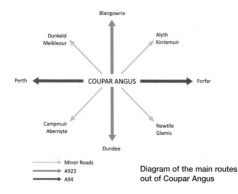

Diagram of the main routes
out of Coupar Angus

Minor Roads
A923
A94

5   The A923 north out of Coupar Angus is relatively busy compared to the
     minor roads around the town, though during weekdays between 9.30 and
     4.30, traffic is pretty light for an A road. The A923 leads ultimately to the
     ski grounds of Glen Shee, Braemar and Aberdeen and is the main road for
     accessing the higher routes on the north side of the Vale of Strathmore.

6   As the A923 leaves Coupar Angus it first climbs a hill then descends over
     the River Isla at Couttie Bridge. Just past the bridge, a minor road goes off
     to the right which is our 6th route out of Coupar Angus. Cycle along the
     minor roads to Ryehill and beyond and where the roads end, a sign-posted
     path to 'Kitty Swanson's Bridge' appears. Take your bike over the bridge
     and follow the path to the north for a short while and you are on minor
     roads which lead to Alyth, the Loch of Lintrathen, Kirriemuir and more.
     You might well wonder who Kitty Swanson was. Kitty ran a ferry across
     the Isla in the early 1800s before the bridge bearing her name was built.

7   If you head out of Coupar Angus in a north-easterly direction, you will follow
     the A94 main road to Glamis and Forfar. As with the A94 to Perth, many of
     our routes cross the Forfar Road but very little cycling is actually done on it.

8   The final route out of Coupar Angus leaves the A94 to Forfar at Larghan
     Park. This minor road heads to Ardler, Meigle, Newtyle, Glamis and lots
     more attractive villages nestling in the shadow of the Sidlaws. It also gives
     access to the B954 over the Sidlaws to Dundee, following the route of an
     old railway line. As you travel round this area, you will see ever increasing
     evidence of the former pre-eminence of the railways.

Also worth mentioning, and a feature of this Strathmore landscape, are the rivers: the Tay, the Isla and the Ericht. Whilst these rivers add hugely to the beauty of the area, they can be annoying if it is a long way to the next bridge. However, when you leave Coupar Angus, the rivers do not present barriers as there are convenient, and often very attractive bridges over each of them.

Routes out of Coupar Angus (Photograph 1 Joe Richards, Coupar Angus)

If you have followed the routes discussed in this section then you will, by now, have no doubt whatsoever that Coupar Angus is the ideal centre for cycle touring in the Vale of Strathmore. You can leave the town by a different road each day for a week and still have one direction left. Furthermore, to the north, south, east and west of Coupar Angus there are minor roads which you can cycle for hours, even in the height of summer, and just see a handful of cars and the odd tractor or two.

All the routes in this guide start from the Cross in the centre of Coupar Angus. You can park near here or, especially if you want to have a meal after your cycle or are staying in the town, there is parking at the Red House (formerly Station Hotel) at the start of the road to Forfar. The initial stages of all the routes are on OS Map 53. For the longer routes, you may want to consult maps 54 and 44. While a smaller scale map is useful, some minor roads may only appear on OS maps. However, ALL of the routes are on the map in the back pocket of this guide book.

Safety on your Bike

Above Murrayshall

The majority of the routes are on minor roads, which are usually very quiet. Some routes, notably those which venture up Glen Shee make some use of 'A' roads, which can be busy. So you always need to take care. It is recommended that you wear a high visibility jacket at all times and a helmet. Perhaps, though, the most significant feature of safety on your bike is ensuring that you are very aware of the traffic around you. Never assume just because you have put on a high visibility jacket, that the traffic will see you. Always assume that the average car driver will not notice you. During all the miles cycled in the preparation of this book, I only ever had one bump from a car. Cycling round a roundabout in Blairgowrie, I assumed that a driver approaching from the left must have seen me, but the driver had not, and the result was a small bump. For all those who say that a cycle helmet is of no use, I was definitely glad I was wearing one. My injuries would have been more severe than a few bruises if I had not. However it did teach me the importance, for cyclists, of assuming the worst when in traffic. Oh, and make sure that your brakes are working well; the Blairgowrie bump could probably have been avoided if I had been able to stop more quickly.

The generally quiet roads around Coupar Angus can lull the cyclist into a false sense of security and it is good to remind yourself, that there could be a boy racer, or a large agricultural vehicle, round the next corner. Fortunately you will almost certainly hear such vehicles before you see them, and can take necessary evasive action. At the time of writing, there are very few 'green' roads (minor roads with a 30 mph speed restriction for the benefit of cyclists) in this book. This is likely to change in the next few years as the popularity of cycling increases and the political pressure for change grows. Some of the 26 routes do interact with national cycle networks and this is noted in the text.

Types of Bike and Bike Accessories

Craigie 1½
Clunie 2

Blairgowrie 4
B947

Spittalfield 1½
Caputh 2½
B947

Some of the Interesting Places you will visit on these Routes

Most of the cycling in this book is on roads, though there are a few miles on tracks. What sort of bike you should use is really a matter of personal preference. You certainly will not need, and would be significantly hampered by, a dedicated off-the-road bike with mega chunky tyres. The choice is probably between an 'all terrain' (ATB) hybrid or an old fashioned touring bike. An ATB would be more stable for covering the miles, but on occasion, for example when bowling up the Glen Shee road and on to Pitlochry, you will be wishing that there was just a little less friction between your tyres and the road. Likewise, on some great descents off the Sidlaws and down into Alyth and the Angus Glens, you might wish you could go faster. A touring bike will deliver speed, with less effort for you. You will certainly need lots of gears to get most enjoyment from the routes. There are some very steep climbs in the Sidlaws and very persistent climbs in the Grampians. Even in the relatively flat Vale of Strathmore you will come across small slopes which, if you are just starting out, might seem significant. The hills will not disappear, however many gears you have, but do become more manageable and less painful with good equipment. If you are going to travel fast, and want to enjoy the most of the downhills, make sure you check your brakes beforehand - something you should do regularly whether or not you are a speed merchant.

Whichever type of bike you choose, you should always carry a spare inner tube, a puncture repair kit and a bicycle pump. You may rarely need them, but sure as fate if you forget to take them with you, you will almost certainly get a puncture. A suitable set of Allen keys is always good to take along plus, in the summer, a reasonable supply of water. On some routes you may be a couple of hours between shops/convenience stores and although there are plenty of tearooms and pubs en route, even these are scarce in some areas. A list of as many of these establishments as can be found in the yellow pages, or are encountered when cycling the routes, is given in the final chapter.

As far as what to wear is concerned, beware, in the east of Perthshire, as in Scotland in general, it can rain any day, so your high visibility jacket needs to be waterproof. Waterproof trousers are recommended unless you are in shorts, and in the autumn, winter and early spring, cycling tights are very common. It CAN be hot, although anyone from a mildly warm country such as southern parts of England/Europe, might dispute this statement. What can be said with some degree of confidence, is that it is never, ever, too hot to cycle in Eastern Perthshire and, if ever it is, I suggest you enjoy the heat, confident in the knowledge that the weather will be back to normal within a day or so. The coolish weather will encourage you to build up the miles. With regard to the wind, a westerly is most common, however, you will soon learn that the wind in Scotland is capricious. The persistent westerly wind you cycled into during the morning is more than capable of turning around through 180° and coming at you from the east as you turn for home, having enjoyed tea and toasties in a comfy Perthshire tearoom.

The ROUTES

Short route with no climbs	Longer route with no climbs	Short route with climbs	Long route with climbs	Long and arduous route

1	**Le Tour de Coupar Angus**	18 miles : 3 hours

Never more than 2.5 miles from Coupar Angus, this cycle introduces the road system around the town and, after crossing Kitty Swanston's Bridge, visits the villages of Ardler, Kettins and Burrelton, before returning on the minor road to Meikleour meeting the A923 back into Coupar Angus.

2	**Over the Sidlaws**	15 miles : 2 hours

To Campmuir, turn left on the road to Abernyte. At the high point of the road turn left to East Newton and right at the next T junction. Turn left after a few hundred metres on the road to Knapp. Turn left just after Knapp to Dron, and turn left in Dron after the church on a track over the hills to meet the minor road to Tullybaccart. At Tullybaccart, take the tracks to the Laird's Loch, around Northballo Hill and turn right on to the minor road to Campmuir. Then back to Coupar Angus. No inns or tearooms but great scenery.

3	**Macbeth's Castle and Dunsinane Hill**	32 miles : 4 hours

A long tour which starts on the road to Campmuir, over the Sidlaws to Abernyte, along beneath the Sidlaws then back over the Sidlaws to Murrayshall past various ancient forts. Back along the Strath to Coupar Angus. Beautiful views and a long hanging valley in the Sidaws make this a memorable excursion. Tearoom at Abernyte (a mile or two off the route), and an inn at Balbeggie.

4	**St Martin's and Waulkmill**	29 miles : 3.5 hours

A94 to Burrelton, leaving Burrelton by the minor road at the end of the village to Strelitz, Cragieholm and then to Guildtown. Turn left on the A93 for 1.5 miles then left to St Martins. Through the village and to Balbeggie, cross the A94 and take the B953 to Bowbridge and turn left for Kinrossie. Then follow the directions for Route 6. Inns in Burrelton and Balbeggie.

| **5** | **Cargill and the Banks of the Tay** | 14 miles : 2 hours |

Out of Coupar Angus on the road to Campmuir. Follow the roads through East Kinnochtry and Burngrange to Redstone. Cross the A94 and up to Craigholme and down to Cargill. Back to the A94 and turn left after just over a mile. Turn right on the road back to Coupar Angus. Inn in Burrelton, possible picnic sites around Cargill.

| **6** | **Stewart Tower Tour** | 25 miles : 3 hours |

Follow Route 2 to just before Kinclaven, there you take the turn for Stanley and Perth. Pass Ballathie and keep going to Stanley. Visit Stanley Mills then retrace route to left turn just outside the village and follow road to Airntully, Cleikiminn and turn left at T junction for Stewart Tower (ice cream stop). Retrace route, avoiding turn to Airntully and turn left at the T junction to Murthly. In the centre of Murthly, take the right turn for Meikleour and return to Coupar Angus via Kinclaven, Tay and Isla Bridges. Shop in Murthly, inns in Stanley and Meikleour, tea room at Stewart Tower.

| **7** | **The Five Lochs Tour** | 33 miles : 3.5 hours |

Take the Blairgowrie Road (A923) and turn left to the cemetery and along Bogside Road. Follow through to the A93, over the Isla and to Meikleour, Lethendy road and Marlee Loch. Through Wester Essendy and Craigie to Loch of Clunie. Continue via Snaigow, Ninewells and Catchpenny to Loch of the Lowes Visitor Centre & Wildlife Reserve. Round to Butterstone Loch and off the main road at Burnside. Back to Clunie then over the hill to Kirkton of Lethendy. Back via Chapel of Lethendy to Meikleour or take the main road. Return the way you came or via the A984 to Coupar Angus. Light refreshments at Loch of the Lowes. Bistro at Butterstone Loch. Inn in Meikleour.

| **8** | **The Roman Camp** | 20 miles : 2 hours |

Start as for Route 3, go past the 'Beech Hedge' to Meikleour but stay on the road to Dunkeld (A984). Where the B947 joins, turn left and go down to the camp.

| **9** | **Coupar Angus to Dunkeld** | 32 miles : 3.5 hours |

Coupar Angus to Dunkeld via Caddam Road, Layston, Isla Bridge, Kinclaven, Murthly, Gettyburn, Byres of Murthly, turn right on to the B867 to the A9 cycle route into Birnam. Into Dunkeld, return via the A984 to Meikleour and A923 Blairgowrie to Coupar Angus road. Things to see: Kinclaven Church, bluebells in Kinclaven, Birnham Institute, cafes, inns and restaurants in Dunkeld, inn in Meikleour.

10   Via Kirkmichael to Pitlochry   58 miles : 6 hours

Start on Route 11 as far as Bridge of Cally where you turn left for Kirkmichael and Enochdhu. When you get to Pitlochry, turn back down the A9 to Dunkeld and pick up the roads in Route 2. This is probably the toughest route in the book but the views more than make up for the effort. Inns in Bridge of Cally and Kirkmichael. All sorts of refreshment in Pitlochry.

11   The Drimmie Loop   22-25 miles : 2-3 hrs

Take the A923 to Blairgowrie and continue on to Bridge of Cally where the road bears to the right. After less than half a mile, turn right to Netherton and climb the hill past Ferns of Cloquhart, Rannagulzion, Coutthill and Bonnington. Eventually this road leads back into Blairgowrie. The normal route back to Coupar Angus is via the A923. Inns, cafés and restaurants in Blairgowrie and an excellent cycle shop.

12   Into the Mountains   31 miles : 3.5 hours

Follow Route 11 but carry on along the A93 for a further 2/3 miles when you turn right past Blackhall Farm and up the side of Drumderg Hill. Carry on past Rannagulzion Farm down a long, long hill to the turn for Tullyfergus and back to Blairgowrie. Alternatively follow the road to Alyth and then to Leitfie, Bardmony over the Isla and back to Coupar Angus via Ardler. Inns, tearooms and restaurants in Blairgowrie, Bridge of Cally, Alyth and Ardler.

13   The High Mountains   43 miles : 4.5 hours

Start as for Route 11 but carry on along the A93 past the turn for Netherton and the turn used in Route 16, then turn right onto a minor road for Blacklunans. The road climbs steeply around the back of Mount Blair and down into the valley of the River Isla. Follow the B951 through Brewlands Bridge where two routes are possible: A) cross the Isla and stay on the B951 to Dykehead where you turn right on to the B954 to Bridge of Craigisla and eventually past Alyth. Then follow Route 16. Alternatively, B) stay on the west side of the Isla at Brewlands Bridge and follow the minor road over the hills to Little Kilry and eventually Bridge of Craigisla. From here there are a number of routes back to Coupar Angus. As well as the facilities mentioned for Route 12, there is an Inn at Kirkton of Glen Isla.

14   To the Lovely Loch of Lintrathen   30 miles : 3 hours

Go to Meigle via Ardler then onto a minor road B954 to Kirriemuir. Leave after a couple of miles, past Ruthven House and Airlie Castle to Loch of Lintrathen. Return to Coupar Angus via Peel Farm, Bridge of Craigisla, a notch in the side of the Hill of Alyth, Alyth, the metal bridge over the Isla and Ardler. Refreshments at Peel Farm and in Meigle, Ardler (may only be in the evenings) and Alyth.

15   Around the Loch of Lintrathen   44 miles : 5 hours

First to Meigle via Ardler and the minor road towards Kirriemuir. At the A928 turn left into Kirriemuir. Leave Kirrie by the B955 Glens Road and turn left to the ford at East Kinwhirrie. Turn left onto a minor road to Balintore then down to Loch of Lintrathen at Pitmudie. Round the loch, either going southwest or east, and join up with Route 14. Back to Coupar Angus via Alyth. Refreshments as for Route 14.

16   Kirriemuir and Peter Pan   38 miles : 4 hours

Follow route 16 until you get to Kirriemuir. Have a look at the Peter Pan statue, JM Barrie's birthplace and the Camera Obscura. Then leave Kirriemuir by the B951 to Kirkton of Kingoldrum and then a minor road to Cairnleith. Back past the Isla gorge and onto a minor road to Alyth. Over the metal bridge and back to Coupar Angus. Lots of tearooms, restaurants and inns in Kirriemuir.

17   The Stones Tour   29 miles : 3.5 hours

Meigle via Ardler. Kirkinch, Kirkton of Nevay, Balkeerie, Eassie and to the A94 at Glamis. Cross the A94 and enter the village. Glamis Castle, Celtic standing stone, St Fergus Well and the Angus Folk Museum. Back to Eassie Farm and the Church (with enclosed Pictish Stone). Cross the Dean Water and back over the hills to Meigle then minor roads to Coupar Angus. Refreshments in Glamis and Meigle.

18   Meigle and Newtyle   17 miles : 2 hours

Over Kitty Swanston's bridge (Route 1). Turn right at the T junction after the bridge then left at the second turning (if you cross the Isla again you have gone too far). Turn right at the next T junction and follow the road to Netherton and Alyth/Meigle road (B954) and turn right. Arriving in Meigle, follow the B954 to Newtyle and the route back to Coupar Angus in Route 12. Inns and tearooms in Meigle and Newtyle.

19   Newtyle and Lundie   25 miles : 2.5 hours

Follow Route 17 to Meigle then join the B954 towards Dundee. Once you are over the watershed, turn west into the Sidlaws till you reach the A923 Dundee to Coupar Angus road. Here there are three choices: 1) Straight down the main road to Coupar Angus. 2) Past the Laird's Loch and on to the Abernyte to Coupar Angus road or, 3) if you are feeling energetic, turn left at Tullybaccart, down to East Newton and then back onto the Abernyte - Coupar Angus road. The third alternative means you cross the watershed three times, and on the third occasion there IS a steep climb.

Inn and tearooms in Meigle and Newtyle and, if you stay on the B954 past the bus shelter you will reach the Pear Tree Restaurant on your left after about half a mile (with no substantial downhills to be reclimbed when you reverse your route back to the bus shelter).

20   Le Tour de Dundee   45 miles : 5 hours

A hybrid route which makes use of the excellent cycle tour around Dundee. First you need to get to the City and this means cycling along the A923 to Camperdown Park on the outskirts of Dundee and then following the well marked trail. The only refreshments on the way to/from Dundee are the irregular Starbucks coffee caravan. Lots of places in the City for refreshments.

21   Through Angus and the Mearns   60 miles : 8 hours

The final route goes via minor roads to Edzell, Laurencekirk and Auchenblae to Stonehaven. The first half takes you to the far east of Strathmore where it joins the area known as 'The Mearns'. As this is a long trip, you will need to catch the train back to Dundee then pedal the 12 miles to Coupar Angus. Coupar Angus to Stonehaven is about 60 miles though you could stop off at Laurencekirk and get the train home. Beware, not many trains stop at Laurencekirk. Refreshments in most of the villages and towns on the route. Although a 60 mile route add on 10 miles travelling back to Coupar Angus.

| 22 | Abernyte Tour | 20 miles : 2.5 hours |

Leave Coupar Angus on the Campmuir Road. Turn left in Campmuir and take the third turning on the right to Kirkton of Collace. Turn left after about 4 miles to Collace and climb past Dunsinane Hill to the B953. Turn left to the village of Abernyte. Retrace your route for half a mile then take a minor road to the right, over a short climb and then back on the road down to Campmuir and then Coupar Angus. Tearoom and craft/antiques centre in Abernyte.

| 23 | Sidlaw Foothills | 7 miles : 45 mins |

Leave Coupar Angus on the Campmuir Road but turn left after half a mile. At the next crossroads turn left and after 1 mile turn left again to the A923. Over the main road and take the first left again after 1 mile. Down the hill to Halliburton House and keep going north till you meet a T junction. Turn left again, through the village of Kettins and turn right onto the A923 to Coupar Angus.

| 24 | Low Level (Flat) Route | 12 miles : 1.5 hours |

Leave Coupar Angus on the A94 east and at Larghan Park, turn right. At the next T junction turn left and follow the road to Ardler then on to Meigle. In Meigle turn right and follow the B954 for about half a mile. Then turn right and soon you are back on the road to Coupar Angus. Tearooms and pubs in Meigle and Ardler.

| 25 | Kitty Swanson's Bridge | 10 miles : 1 hour |

Take the A923 out of Coupar Angus and the first right after the Isla Bridge. Stay on the same road till you get to a T junction at Ryehill, turn left then right after 100 yards. Cycle or walk along the track to Kitty Swanson's Bridge. Cross the bridge and turn left. At the next T junction turn right and, after 1.5 miles cross the Isla again and eventually reach the A94. Turn left, then right to Ardler. Turn right in Ardler and take the road back to Coupar Angus.

| 26 | Stormont Loch and the Gull Colony | 10 miles : 1 hour |

A short tour, starting on the A923, half way to Blair turn left to Stormont Loch. Through the woods to Hare Myre Loch and the gull colony. Same way back to Coupar Angus or cross the A923 to Ryehill and reverse Le Tour de Coupar Angus. No refreshments en route.

1   Le Tour de Coupar Angus   18 miles : 3 hours

Written in 'real time' - yesterday Bradley Wiggins won the Tour de France. This momentous achievement needs to be recorded somehow in this book. A Tour de Strathmore is possible but it is very wet (it is the Summer of 2012) so a smaller, more intimate Tour de Coupar Angus beckons. This is a relatively short route, suitable for an evening or afternoon. It is based around the eight roads that leave Coupar Angus and you will get to cycle on, or cross, all of them. This route starts with the crossing of Kitty Swanston's Bridge and a short piece of the route here cannot be cycled. So be prepared to push!

The Start of the Cycle Routes

Leave Coupar Angus on the main A923 north to Blairgowrie. Less than a mile out, you cross the River Isla on the Couttie Bridge and a short distance later there is a crossroads, turn right. The road meanders along for a mile or two when you get to the Model Cottages on your left and a spur on the right to Ryehill. Turn left at this point to a sharp left in the road. A sign points on the right to the River Ericht Path and Kitty Swanson's Bridge. Take this path, cycling as far as you can then pushing.

Kitty Swanson's Bridge

Over the bridge you turn left on a track next to the river. Follow this till you reach a minor road where you turn right. This road slowly turns south east, crosses the 'Metal Bridge' (as the bridge over the Dean Water is known) and eventually reaches the A94 Coupar Angus to Forfar road. Turn left and immediately right following the signs to 'P. Grewar Potatoes'. (Is this the only sign in the UK to a potato farm?) Strathmore is a particularly important seed potato growing area. This road also leads to the small village of Ardler where you turn right (noting the pub on the other side of the road). A short way along this road you will see a left turn to the village of Kettins; take this turn and when you arrive at Keillor House (note the dovecote or doocot), turn right again and soon you will be in Kettins. Kettins must be the smallest village in Scotland with its own bypass. Past Kettins you soon reach the A923 from Coupar Angus to Dundee. Cross over the road and turn left at the next T junction.

The 'Metal' Bridge

The Tavern at Ardler

Now you skirt around Lintrose House and come to a crossroads, turn right (again) to Campmuir and to the A94 Coupar Angus to Perth road at Woodside. Cross the road and go about a mile and half along a minor road to Cargill and Meikleour till you reach a cemetery. Turn right here and follow the road back into Coupar Angus. When you reach a T junction in the town, turn left down Buttery Bank till you meet the A94 Coupar Angus to Blairgowrie road again where, for the last time, you turn right, back up to Coupar Angus.

On this route you will have cycled along or crossed, each of the eight ways out of Coupar Angus. Every other route in the book starts off on one of these.

The Red House in Coupar Angus is a good starting point for many of the routes. It has an extensive car park and accommodation as well as meals and drinks. There are a variety of other pubs and eateries in Coupar Angus including an Indian restaurant and the 'Y' Community Café. There is also a Scotmid supermarket for all your drinks, snacks and provisions. The final chapter lists other tearooms, pubs, inns and other accommodation in the area around Coupar Angus.

Into the Tay Valley

Route 2 is not long but contains the steepest climb in this book. Although it is not a long climb, the gradient is very severe. Start slowly, getting into a very low gear and you will be fine. If you have to walk, so be it, you won't be the only one who has been defeated by this pass over the usually gentle Sidlaws. A little bit of perspective – Glasgow has its Campsie Fells, Edinburgh has its Pentland Hills, Aberdeen doesn't actually have any hills, but Dundee has its Sidlaws (Sidlees to the locals).

Leave Coupar Angus by the second route out of the town, via Campmuir. When you reach this village turn left and head for the hills. Half a mile south of Campmuir, the 'main' road turns sharply to the right but you need to go straight on. At first the road climbs gently but ultimately becomes very steep. At the top of the hill, stop to catch your breath and have it taken away again by the views to the north. Your route carries on downhill into a valley in the Sidlaws and up the other side (not so steep). At the top of the second hill you turn left down a very steep incline and come to a T junction where you turn left and climb the Sidlaws once more.

The Laird's Loch

The road you are on now meets the main Dundee to Coupar Angus road at Tullybaccart where, if you are lucky, there may be a refreshment caravan. Cycle into the carpark on the left and you will see a track that leads to another of the area's beautiful lochs. Go round the north side of this Laird's Loch then turn left onto a track which winds around the south side of the hills and eventually leads you out at the top of the very steep hill above Campmuir. Turn right down the hill and retrace your route to Campmuir and Coupar Angus.

A trip to one of Scotland's most charismatic hill forts, known locally as 'MacBeth's Castle'. The fort was built in the Iron Age and you approach it from the small village of Collace, the first destination on this route. The fort ramparts still exist and if you climb to the top, 308 meters above sea level, you will cross many of them, to be rewarded with great views across the Vale of Strathmore. As Shakespeare has MacBeth say, in the play of the same name, 'I will not be afraid of death and bane till Birnam Forest come to Dunsinane'. Whether or not Dunsinane Hill has any other connections to MacBeth is not known but it is certainly true that on a clear day, you can see Birnam Wood (just outside Dunkeld).

Leave Coupar Angus by route 2 to Campmuir and when you reach the T junction turn left. After about 1.5 miles take a right turn on the road to Collace. After about 3 miles on this very minor road you will reach a crossroad with a left turn to Collace. At the end of the village there is a footpath to the top of Dunsinane Hill and this is the best way up. The road climbs up the side of the hill, passes a quarry that looks as if it will finally remove Dunsinane Hill and MacBeth's curse as well, and reaches a T junction where, as long as you are feeling fit, turn left and go up a gentle hill on the B953 to Abernyte. Just past Abernyte is a restaurant and craft/antique centre which is worth a visit.

The Sidlaw Hills

After suitable refreshment go back to the school in Abernyte and turn left along the back road to Fingask and Rait. This road descends into the valley of the River Tay, known as the Carse of Gowrie. An upward slow road takes you past Fingask Castle, Rait and its antiques centre, through Kilspindie and to a right turn to Murrayshall. Here the going gets tough as you climb a steep hill to reach the floor of an attractive hanging valley in the Sidlaws. If you stop to look over your shoulder, you will be rewarded with great views of the Tay Estuary and finally at the top of the valley, equally great views across Strathmore to Schiehallion, Beinn a'Ghlo and the mountains around Glen Shee. Coming down into Strathmore, you will pass Murrayshall Golf Club and hotel (for a meal or a drink) to reach the A94 at Gretnagreen Farm (opposite Perth Aerodrome). Here you need to turn right and follow the main road for about 1.5 miles. The A94 is busy but there is a rarely used footpath on the west side of the road.

North Across Strathmore

At Balbeggie (MacDonald Arms Hotel) you bear right at the fork onto the B953 to Abernyte (you joined this road earlier just past Dunsinane Hill), turning left at a fork after about 2 miles. The road will take you round to the small village of Kinrossie. Past the village, you come to a slightly distorted crossroads where you go straight across another minor road bearing slightly left. At the next T junction turn left again and after half a mile, turn right at another T junction. You are now on the road back to Campmuir. Keep going north east till the T junction where you turn left and Campmuir will appear in less than half a mile. Turn right in Campmuir and head back to Coupar Angus.

A long start to this tour, but once you are underway the interest heightens. Refreshments are available and the farthest point of the route is an excellent picnic spot with kindly provided picnic table and chairs.

Firstly you need to get to Burrelton. Either take the A94 from Coupar Angus or Caddam Road, the fourth route out of Coupar Angus (see chapter on Coupar Angus as a Centre for Cycle Touring). If you take Caddam Road, about a mile from the town, it right angles to the right. Turn left here, through Mains of Keithick Farm and down to the A94. Turn right, either on to the road or the overgrown footpath. Go through Woodside and then at the end of Burrelton, you will see another right turn to Strelitz and Wolfhill. This road, Whitelea Road, climbs steadily and comes out on a plateau from which you can see the Cairngorms (on the right), the mountains Stuc a 'Chroin and Ben Vorlich (to the west) and the Sidlaws (to the south). The plateau feels very light and airy with huge skies on a clear day.

Eventually the road turns downhill towards Guildtown and when you reach the main A93, turn right and after a few hundred yards, turn left towards Stormontfield. From here the road descends into the valley of the Tay. When you get to Stormontfield Church you can turn right, through a new village and then bear left along a fine road next to a flood channel of the Tay. Turn right just before you rejoin the 'main' road to Waulkmill. Alternatively, carry on along the main road till you meet the private road to Colenhaugh. Turn left, then immediately left to Waulkmill where there used to be a ferry across the Tay.

The Tay at Waulkmill

From Waulkmill retrace your route to Stormontfield Road and continue in a south easterly direction, past Perth Race Course until you meet the A93 Perth to Braemar road again. Turn left, pass the Strawberry Shop and, after 2.5 miles, you will see a right turn to St Martins. Take this turning.

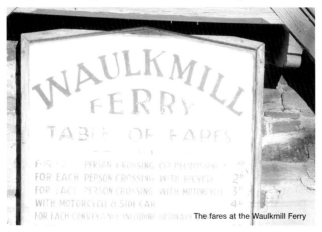
The fares at the Waulkmill Ferry

When you reach St Martins, there is a choice of two routes: either continue on the minor road to Balbeggie and then Route 3 (MacBeth's Castle at Dunsinane) home to Coupar Angus. Or, for a more sporting route, take the minor track to St Martins Church, follow the track up the hill past the Church to Kinswell where it starts to get rather overgrown. Keep going straight along the track, ignoring routes off to the left, and eventually, after maybe some pushing, you reach Garden Cottage and then Dunsinnan House. When you reach the metalled road to the house, turn right down to the A94 where you turn left. Again there are two choices: either continue on the A94 to Coupar Angus or, after three quarters of a mile, take a right turn to Kinrossie and Collace and follow Route 3 back to Coupar Angus.

Refreshments are limited to Burrelton or Balbeggie. Though you are never far from the main A roads, some parts of this route seem really isolated. You will see very few cars, just some tractors at harvest time.

If time is pressing, or legs are tired, this route can be shortened by leaving out the loop to Stormontfield. However, in my opinion, this misses out the most interesting and picturesque part of the whole tour.

This tour goes to the tiny hamlet of Cargill on the banks of the River Tay.
The route includes some stunning views of central Scotland but is a bit short
on refreshments!

Go south out of central Coupar Angus on the Dundee Road and, almost
immediately after the 'relief road' turn right for Campmuir. At the T junction in
Campmuir turn left and at the next crossroads, turn right through Kinnochtry,
Burngrange and Lawton to Redstone on the A94. Cross the main road and go
up the hill to the crossroads at Craigieholme. Go straight over to a magnificent
view of central Scotland then down a steep, steep hill (TAKE CARE) to the A93
at the bottom. Go straight over the A93 and down to Cargill. If you get off your
bike in the village and go through the graveyard, with a bit of scrambling, you
can get down to the banks of the Tay. To your right is a disused railway bridge
on the line from Perth to Coupar Angus. On the bike once more, follow the
road round till you meet the A93 again. Turn left onto what, although it is not
a busy road, does seem to attract fast drivers! After about 1 mile you will need
to turn right (signposted Burrelton) and carry on up the hill and down the other
side till you get to the cemetery described in Route 2. Here you turn left off the
Burrelton road (actually straight on) and keep going straight until after a couple
of miles you get to a T junction back in Coupar Angus.

Fungi and Honeysuckle at Cargill

Unfortunately, apart from a pub in Burrelton and tearooms, pubs etc. in Coupar
Angus, the rest of this route is refreshment free.

This is an interesting tour, particularly if you include the side excursions to Ballathie House Hotel, Stanley Mills and the Church at Kinclaven. The route follows mostly B-roads or less, though one or two are relatively busy. So bright, reflective clothes are recommended.

Leave Coupar Angus by Route 4, the A923 to Blairgowrie, take the road to the left soon after the roundabout (sign-posted to the Cemetery). Along Bogside Road, left and soon right at the end and on to Caddam Road. Keep going along this road and after 2 miles, you reach a second cemetery, where you turn right onto the road from Woodside. Carry on for another mile or two till you reach the A93 Perth to Blairgowrie road. Turn right and over the Isla Bridge and then, almost immediately, turn left and over the River Tay.

After half a mile you come to a left turn signposted to Perth (12 miles). Interestingly the sign also suggests that it is 12 miles along the road you have just cycled, to Perth. Quite who would need to know this, is beyond me. Presumably only someone who was lost, and had travelled the wrong way, would be interested. So maybe this is a sign for lost travellers, or the sign writer was just having a wee joke!

About 1 mile along the road to Perth (the one you have just turned onto) you will see an entrance to Ballathie House Hotel (you will already have passed the tradesman's entrance). Turn left down to the hotel for lunch, high tea or dinner. If you cycle past the hotel you can get down to the Tay for an interesting view of Cargill and the old rail bridge. You may also see people fishing in the Tay but, if you want to join them, it will probably cost considerably more than you paid for your bike (unless it is a Tour de France racer).

Ballathie House by the Tay

Retrace your route to the 'main' road and turn left. After 3 miles you reach the B9099, turn left towards Stanley and at the entrance to the village, turn left down past Tayside Hotel and carry on down the hill to the faithfully restored Stanley Mills. With the restoration undertaken by Historic Scotland, the Mill is a really fine link to the industrial revolution, a time when sustainable energy fuelled many of our factories!

Stanley Mill

After a tour of the Mill, cycle back up the hill to B9099 and turn right. Just out of Stanley you will see a turn on the left to Airntully, which gets you off the relatively busy B-road and onto an unclassified minor road. After going through the village, look to your left and you will see Stewart Tower Dairy, the farthest point of this route. Turn left at the T junction and along to the Stewart Tower tea-room and farm shop, and source of Perthshire's best known home-made ice cream.

Go back down to the B9099 and turn left along to Murthly, where you will see a right turn to Kinclaven. Follow this road over a level crossing and past the Druids Park luxury housing development. After about 3 miles, on your right you will pass the bluebell woods (visit in late April or May depending on whether it is an early or late season) and on the left, a side road takes you down to Kinclaven Church. Back on the main road

you will pass the dual sign to Perth and from now on you are retracing the outward route – over the Tay, over the Isla, past the cemetery and eventually back into Coupar Angus.

Apart from ice cream at Stewart Tower, refreshments are available in Stanley and Murthly.

Loch of the Lowes

This route shows the full beauty of Strathmore, lochs, wildlife (including deer, red squirrels and ospreys), heather covered mountains, churches and beautiful houses.

Leave Coupar Angus on the A923 to Blairgowrie and take the roads described in Route 6, the Stewart Tower tour. When you reach the A93 to Blairgowrie, go over the Isla Bridge but stay on this road, past the famous Meikleour Beech Hedge. The Beech Hedge was planted in 1745 and is one third of a mile long and 30 metres (100ft) high. Not surprisingly the hedge is in the Guinness Book of Records – the largest hedge in the whole world! At the end of the hedge, turn left into the pretty little village of Meikleour, noting the attractive pub for later. Take the road to Lethendy at the end of the village. When you join the B947 go straight on down the hill and turn left for Craigie. As you climb up the hill you can glimpse the first loch, Marlee Loch. Soon you will arrive at Loch of Clunie, where you turn left. At the end of the loch turn right to visit the church at Clunie.

Clunie Church

Across Clunie Loch

Up another hill and straight across at a crossroads takes you to Snaigow, where you turn right and down the hill to Loch of the Lowes. You will be close to Butterstone Loch here but there is no access from this side of the loch. Beside Loch of the Lowes there is an excellent centre operated by Scottish Wildlife Trust and where snacks are available.

Nesting by this loch, as they have been for the past 26 years, is a pair of ospreys and there are hides complete with binoculars and a telescope for observing these exciting birds. You may be lucky enough to see them fishing. Red squirrels abound around the visitor centre along with lots of other birds and even otters. Take time to enjoy Loch of the Lowes before you head back.

Loch of the Lowes

These are quiet roads, on a sunny day in mid-July I met 3 cars, a timber lorry and a milk van doing its rounds on the 6 miles from the B947 to Loch of the Lowes. Leave the loch and go right onto the A923 towards Blairgowrie. Stay on this road till Butterstone Loch (you will pass Loch of Craiglush, the fourth loch on this tour), where there is a great bistro. For the bistro, turn right off the road and about 300 yards down to the fifth loch of the tour (Butterstone).

Continue on the A923 to Burnside (on the same July day, I met 4 cars and a camper van), then turn right and follow the signs back to Clunie then Craigie. Turn right as you leave Craigie and follow the road to Kirkton of Lethendy. Here you can turn left, and after about 1 mile turn right and follow the route you started out on. Alternatively, turn left to the A984 and follow the signs back to Coupar Angus (A984 followed by right turn at A923). If you are tired, the second route has no hills! Either way you will pass the excellent pub in Meikleour.

Autumn Colours

The Roman Camp Route is really just a side-route off the next route, Coupar Angus to Dunkeld. However it is sufficiently far off the main road, and sufficiently interesting, to merit its own route. If having done it you are full of energy and raring to go, then just continue along Route 9, to Dunkeld.

Start as for the 'Five Lochs Tour' but follow the main road out of Meikleour till you reach the junction with the B947 to Kirkton of Lethendy (a right hand turn off the main road). Opposite this road, on your left, you will see a minor road-sign pointing to the Roman Camp. Turn down this road, past Nether Aird Farm till you reach the banks of the Tay. Here the road bears right, past a house with a huge walled garden (Delvine Gardens) and up to the Roman Camp. There is a fair amount to see here as the fortress, constructed around AD 83, has never been built over. Indeed if you walk on past the site of the fort, you come up to a large raised plateau, and it is possible, with a fair amount of imagination, to see the Roman troops training in this rather special place. Perhaps the most unusual find when the fortress, known to the Romans as Pinnata Castra, was excavated in the 1950s - 1960s, was a hoard of 750,000 iron nails, apparently hidden to prevent them being used by the natives, (see http://www.romanscotland.org.uk/pages/narratives/nailhoard.asp). The surrounding area is called Inchtuthil.

Near the Roman Camp

Retracing your route down to Delvine
Gardens, it is just a short trek over one
field to the banks of the Tay where there
is an excellent picnic spot. The river
is prone to flooding in very wet weather
but normally it is possible to get to the
river bank with dry feet. After your picnic,
retrace your route past Nether Aird Farm
and back to the Dunkeld road, where you
can either turn right and head directly
back to Coupar Angus, go straight across
to Kirkton of Lethendy, or turn left and join

Map of the Camp

Route 9. If you take the second option, turn right (follow the road around) at
Kirkton, turn left (follow the road around) at Chapel of Lethendy and eventually
reach the A93 Perth to Blairgowrie road. Turn right and after less than half a
mile, turn left on Golf Course Road. Eventually this reaches the A923 Coupar
Angus to Blairgowrie road where you turn right, over the Isla Bridge and back
to Coupar Angus.

Apart from the pub in Meikleour, this route is refreshment free unless you make
a short detour into Blairgowrie.

Mist in the Tay Valley

This route follows three old and modern transport routes through Scotland, the River Tay, the main railway line to Inverness and the A9 dual carriageway to Inverness. You will cross the Tay twice, go under the A9 twice and cross the railway line at a level crossing (once), under two bridges and over the line once. This is all on the way to Dunkeld. The route back follows the Tay to Meikleour then switches to the Isla.

Leave Coupar Angus by the A923 to Blairgowrie, turning left to the cemetery and follow The Five Lochs Tour till you cross the Isla Bridge. Turn left after the bridge and cross the bridge over the River Tay. Continue on this road past Kinclaven and over the level crossing at Murthly. At the T junction turn left.

🚲 CYCLISTS 🚲

Before crossing, wait for new turn of lights. Cycle over loops cut into the road surface to extend the time of the green light.

Confusing Sign

Half a mile after the railway bridge in Murthly, a left fork signposted to Pittensorn is the route and the road closes in on the railway line for a couple of miles. Eventually the road goes over the line, just before it enters a tunnel and ends at a T junction B867 Bankfoot to Dunkeld road. Turn right. Down the hill, under the railway line again till you reach the A9 then go onto the cycle path past Dunkeld Station. A low bridge takes you under the main road and delivers you onto the old A9 in Birnam. If you fancy a coffee, turn right for the interesting Birnam Institute and Beatrix Potter garden, otherwise turn left to the T junction and right over the Wade Bridge across the Tay and into Dunkeld.

Back Street Dunkeld

After a break in Dunkeld you have three possible routes back:

Route 1: Continue along Dunkeld High Street till you reach the right turn for the A923 to Blairgowrie. Follow the road up, initially a very steep hill to Blairgowrie then turn south onto the A923 to Coupar Angus.

Route 2: As for Route 1 but turn off the A923 at Burnside and follow the 5 Lochs route.

Route 3: Go back to the Wade Bridge but turn left just before it onto the A984 to Meikleour. At Meikleour (about 11 miles), turn left and follow the A984 back to Coupar Angus. Route 3 is my favourite mainly because the hill on the A923 leaving Dunkeld is just too steep.

Tay Bridge Dunkeld

Tearoom and pubs in Birnam and Dunkeld and a pub in Meikleour make this a well serviced route. There is also a small shop in Murthly.

North of Bridge of Cally

The route to Pitlochry takes you into the heart of tourist Scotland. Pitlochry has lots of cafés and tearooms, lots of pubs and shops, and lots and lots of people and cars. Entering Pitlochry after a couple of hours cycling the roads of Strathmore can be something of a culture shock. However the tour up Strathardle is too good to miss.

Start the route on the A923 to Blairgowrie and carry on along the A93 to Bridge of Cally with its hotel, post office and fishing book shop. A full description of this route is given in the next chapter. At Bridge of Cally you leave the roads for Glen Shee and turn left on the A924 up Strathardle. The A924 is a delight, a good, well surfaced road with hardly any traffic and beautiful Perthshire scenery. The Strath has four notable villages, Ballintuim, Kirkmichael, Enochdu and Straloch (more of a hamlet). Of the three, Kirkmichael is perhaps the most interesting with its various pubs. Take a moment to cross over the river Ardle to see the village from the bridge.

Strathardle

The Moulin Hotel

As you carry on up the Strath, Ben Vrackie starts to dominate the scene. This is the pointed mountain that overlooks Pitlochry and is often seen in photographs of the town. About four miles past Straloch you will see a war memorial to the right of the road. Great photos of Ben Vrackie from around here. Soon after this comes the steepest part of the road, followed by a short, high level plateau before the long descent to Pitlochry. Just before reaching the town, you will pass through the village of Moulin which sports a hotel with its own microbrewery.

Into Pitlochry and navigation becomes a little difficult. You need to take the A9 towards Perth and almost immediately you go under the main railway line, turning right at the sign Pitlochry Festival Theatre. You cross the River Tummel then turn left on the minor road to Ballinluig. This road joins the A827 Ballinluig to Aberfeldy road where you turn left, over the A9 and into Ballinluig.

There is an alternative route to Ballinluig, which is very scenic but rather hilly. Start as in the previous paragraph but carry on along the road towards the A9 till you see a road off to the left, signposted Balchandy. (In other words DON'T turn right to the Festival Theatre.) This road goes under the railway and after a couple of miles you turn left up a steep and long hill to Balchandy. The road carries on up to Milton of Dalcapon, with beautiful views across Strathtay till you get to a T junction (another couple of miles). Turn right down into Ballinluig.

The cycle track (A88) to Perth leaves central Ballinluig via a right turn and down beside the A9. You will go under the A827. Be careful on this track; it feels like a route just for cycles but cars use it occasionally. From here on you follow the cycle track signs to Dowally and Rotmell Farm where a minor road goes off left and follows the A9 into Dunkeld. Here you join the A923 and turn right for Dunkeld, or left up the hill, for Loch of the Lowes, Blairgowrie and Coupar Angus. The left turn is not recommended if the route has been tough, so go into Dunkeld and follow the A984 back to Meikleour and Coupar Angus.

Near Kirkmichael

The total distance is about 60 miles. There are plenty of sights on the way, from the salmon fish ladder and distillery at Pitlochry to the Dirnanean gardens at Enochdu in Strathardle. Refreshments are available in Blairgowrie, Bridge of Cally, Kirkmichael, Moulin, Pitlochry, Ballinluig, Dowally, Dunkeld and Meikleour, so on a sunny summer's day, this route can take quite a while.

Drimmie Village

This and the next two routes all start with a dash up the main A93 to Bridge of Cally. The Drimmie Loop has lovely views but this route is really an escape plan for those who look at the mountains ahead with trepidation. Still, if you can manage this route, maybe this will give you confidence for the more challenging trips ahead.

So, leave Coupar Angus on the A93 to the attractive town of Blairgowrie where you follow the A93, now signposted Braemar, north out of the town. After following the river Ericht for a while, the road crosses the river and sets off up the first climb of the day on a new road. (Look out for views of Craighall, a house to your right on the other side of the Ericht. The original A93 has been by-passed here because of an unsafe, for cars, bridge. The road is safe for cyclists and gives great views of Craighall mansion and the gorge of the Ericht. You access the old road just out of Blairgowrie by a turn to the right immediately after the road crosses the Ericht). Returning to the main route, unfortunately soon after completing the arduous climb out of Blairgowie there is a steep descent into Bridge of Cally where most of the height gained is lost. Stay on the Braemar road at Bridge of Cally and soon a road appears on the right signposted Drimmie. Take this road, cross the Ericht in a very small hamlet and start up the long hill to Milton of Drimmie. The first hill slackens off quickly, but there is a steeper one to come! At the highest point, next to Drimmie Forest, a great descent starts, which passes standing stones near Courthill where you can see the spires of Craighall again. Above Craighall you will find the mountains Stuc A'Chroin, Ben Vorlich, Ben Vrackie and the long ridge of Beinn a'Ghlo (Route 10 follows along the base of this mountain).

North to the Mountains

At the bottom of the hill you will be back in Blair (as it is known to locals) and the A923 back to Coupar Angus beckons.

If you don't fancy the main road, turn off left to Tesco just after the Ericht Bridge and follow the minor road ahead to a T junction. Turn left, past the Coop Fruit Farms, bear right after about a mile and left at the next T junction. Follow the road ahead as it does a big loop to the right and eventually you will come out at the Couttie Bridge over the River Isla, just before Coupar Angus. This route can also be used, in reverse, to get to Blairgowrie but it is a slow start if you are on a long cycle.

If you are feeling really adventurous and have an ATB, when you get to Blair at the start of Route 11, turn left on the A93 and then right onto the A923 to Dunkeld. When you reach the hamlet of Kinloch (about 1.5 miles) a minor road goes off to the right over the hills to Bridge of Cally. Up until the Lornty Burn this is a metalled road but soon after it becomes more of a farm track and eventually an old military road. You will be rewarded with tremendous views and a great feeling of isolation.

Lots of interest on this route. Blair has many pub and restaurants, there is a pub in Bridge of Cally and a fishing book shop. After that, the roads are quiet and there are no more refreshments till you are back in Blair.

Glen Shee

Route 12 is the shortest route in this guide which gives a real feel for the mountains. Unfortunately it includes two serious climbs, the A93 just north of Blairgowrie and the minor road over Drumderg Hill. The views from Drumderg are very extensive and just a short walk off the road is a viewpoint where you will feel as if you are in the heart of the mountains. With views to the south and west over Strathmore and the Sidlaws this is one of the best routes from which to understand the scale of Strathmore. But unless your hill climbing skills have been honed this will be a taxing route for you. Drumderg is the site of the largest wind farm in this part of Scotland and you will get glimpses of the windmills all along the route.

BLEATON HALLET
PRIVATE

Bleaton Hallet

The Drumderg Windmills

The trip starts as for Routes 10 and 11. Go through Bridge of Cally, staying on the A93. Go a couple of miles past the road for Drimmie to the next turning on the right, signposted for Tullymurdoch and Alyth. This is your route. The road crosses the Shee Water, goes past the curiously named Bleaton Hallet (sounds as if it has escaped from Somerset) and then starts on the long climb up Drumderg Hill. The first part of the hill has sharp bends in it but, as you get into the open moorland, the road straightens and you will see the windfarm straight in front. Just before the top of the hill a path goes off to the left to a very impressive viewpoint. Over the brow of the hill you will pass a road on your right, get back below the tree line and see a road on the left to Glen Isla and, at the bottom of the hill, your road turns off to the right to Tullyfergus and St Fink. The road crosses the top of the attractive Alyth Den, climbs up once again and then descends to Rattray on the A926 Alyth to Blairgowrie road. Turn right and in a few minutes you will be back in the centre of Blairgowrie.

If you can't face the final climb to Tullyfergus then stay on the road into Alyth and follow Route 13 back to Coupar Angus. Refreshments are to be found in Blairgowrie and Bridge of Cally and, if you miss out the final hill, in Alyth.

47

The Black Water

Make no mistake, this is a hard route with a tough start. The far point of the ride gets into the upper reaches of Glen Isla, the most westerly, and some would say the most beautiful of the Angus Glens. After the tough hills at the start of the route, the road through the Glen is a joy and the views are exceptional.

Start as for Routes 10, 11 and 12 and bear right at Bridge of Cally. Now stay on the A93 road to Braemar, past the alternative route to Pitlochry (B950) and after another mile, turn right on the minor road to Blacklunans. After half a mile turn left, unless you are struggling, in which case stay on the main road and rejoin Route 13 at Brewlands Bridge. After about 2 miles you will get to the small hamlet of Cray where you turn right on to the B951 to Glen Isla. Going up this road you might expect a steep climb as you are moving from one extensive valley to the next. Surprisingly there is hardly any climbing, maybe 20 or 30 meters, and soon you are bowling down into Glen Isla. Look out for the attractive castle at Forter. Keep on the main road when you reach the turn to Folda and Auchavan, unless you fancy a trip up the Glen, and cross the Isla at Brewlands Bridge. (Alternatively keep the Isla on your left and follow the road over the hills till you get to B954 just south of Bridge of Craigisla.)

Glen Isla

The main route keeps the Isla on your right, passes Glen Isla Hotel and turns right at Dykend where there is a short road on the left going to the Backwater Reservoir. Just after Glen Isla Hotel, keep an eye out for the rather extravagant circular house at Knockshannoch where the Highland Adventure Centre is based. The B954 eventually meets the road from Loch of Lintrathen (and Peel Farm) where you turn right. Follow the road down to the main A926 (Blairgowrie to Kirriemuir road) keeping to the east of Alyth. At the junction with the A926 (a five exit roundabout), take the third exit to Meigle. Turn left at the A94 and into Meigle where you turn right onto the B954 (again). Almost immediately turn right off the B954 following the signs to Ardler. Minor roads take you back to Coupar Angus.

The route is just over 40 miles but feels more. The A93 out of Blairgowrie is particularly punishing and the hardest climb on the whole route comes just after you cross the River Ericht for the second time. If you get up this hill in one piece, then the rest of the hills, though arduous, are a doddle. None are that long, they are just disturbingly frequent.

Refreshments are available in Blairgowrie, too early to be much use, at Glen Isla Hotel (check opening hours) and in Alyth if you take a short detour into the town.

As with many cities in Scotland, when Dundee needed water in the 19th century for the industrial revolution, it looked to the hills, and the lovely Loch of Lintrathen is the result. Whilst still used as a water supply, the loch is also a major wildlife centre run by Scottish Wildlife Trust who also look after the ospreys at Loch of the Lowes. About 16 miles from Coupar Angus, the Loch of Lintrathen route traverses a wide variety of different scenery with a number of steep, if relatively short, hills. This is one of my favourite trips, with tearooms, pubs and restaurants along the way and views of lochs, forests, hills and some of the grander Scottish mountains.

Scottish Wildlife Trust: http://scottishwildlifetrust.org.uk/reserve/loch-of-lintrathen/

Start by cycling to Meigle via Ardler (see The Stones Tour, route 17). When you reach Meigle, turn left into the village, left onto the A94 back to Coupar Angus, then right as you leave the village on the road to Alyth (B954) and immediately right again on a minor road signposted Kirriemuir 10 miles. This attractive wee road soon crosses the Dean Water, a major tributary of the Isla (note the exquisite estate bridge just upstream) and, after about another two miles you turn left to Ruthven, Airlie and Lintrathen. The road coasts along for a mile till you reach the main A926 Blairgowrie to Kirriemuir road. Cross this road and start to climb slowly, then more steeply once you pass a side road to Alyth up the side of the gorge which contains the River Isla, the Reekie Linn. This gorge contains lots of waterfalls and a view of the lower part is visible from the bridge on the road to Alyth.

Loch of Lintrathen

The road goes up and up, leaves the Isla for a while, goes down to Melgam Water (from the Loch of Lintrathen) and then goes up again till you arrive at the old Lintrathen Primary School. A few yards on you will get your first view of the Loch of Lintrathen and what a peaceful and scenic view it is. The backdrop to the loch is a ring of relatively low hills but with grander mountains peeping through some of the gaps in the foothills. A quick ride down the last hill brings you to the loch. Suddenly you start to feel as if you are on the edge of the real Highlands.

Turn left when you reach the shore of the loch and in about a mile you get to the new Lintrathen School and, next door, the very attractive Peel Farm craft shop and, very welcome, tearoom. If you look south as you ride to Peel Farm you will see a relatively low ridge of hills, the Hill of Alyth. This ends in a small blimp, Barry Hill (and fort) and your road is going to go over the small pass between Alyth and Barry Hills. You will hardly notice the climb from this side but the run down to Alyth is very exhilarating. Don't take the right turn, just past the Loch of Lintrathen, for Balintore, this is a cycle for another day. From Peel Farm you can access the upper reaches of the Reekie Linn as well as enjoy excellent home baking.

Peel Farm Tearoom

The 'Notch' above Alyth

On the road again you soon reach the B954 to Alyth. After the small pass beside Barry Hill (worth quickly climbing if the weather is clear for an outstanding view of the Highlands), the B954 becomes the B952 and, ignoring a sign for Dundee, follow the 952 into the town. On the right you will pass the entrance to the very grand Lands of Loyal Hotel, worth visiting for a cup of tea or a meal. Alyth is a bit confusing as the Alyth Burn, another tributary of the Isla, runs through the centre of town. You need to cross the burn then follow the signs for Blairgowrie till you meet the A926. Turn right and take the first turn on the left to Leitfie and Strathmore Golf Club. A beautifully situated golf course, the road runs between the fairways until you reach a crossroad just before Leitfie. Turn right and very soon you will sight the metal bridge which features on 'Le Tour de Coupar Angus'. You need to cross this bridge, up to the A94, turn left then right and into Ardler. Then retrace your steps to Coupar Angus. All in all about 30 interesting miles full of diversity.

The Ford at Kinwhirrie

Make no mistake, this is a tough cycle. The initial ride to Kirriemuir is sweetness and light. The trek from Kirriemuir to Balintore is very hard work and included one of the very few places that I decided to walk my bike. (In defence, I was nursing the early stages of pleurisy.) Nevertheless, that I needed to walk does reflect the up and down nature of the route. Fortunately the ride to Balintore is full of interest and the route from Balintore back to Coupar Angus, described in Route 14, is easy and includes one of the best tearooms in the district at Peel Farm.

Leave Coupar Angus heading for Meigle via Ardler. When you reach Meigle, turn onto the A94 back to Coupar Angus and turn right, and right again, as soon as you leave the village. You are now on a minor road that goes nearly all the way to Kirriemuir. (It is the same road that you would have started on if you had done Route 14.) Eventually, after 4 or 5 miles, this road meets a T junction where you turn left onto the A928 and up the hill into Kirriemuir.

Kirriemuir is quite a complex town with a sort of by-pass to the west which is signposted 'To The Glens'. Whilst this is actually the direction you need, it is more interesting to cycle into the centre of the town, past the Peter Pan statue. Again you will see a road signposted The Glens (Glen Isla and Glen Prosen) and you follow this road, the B953 out of town. After about a mile, the road turns sharply right (to the east) and there is a road on the left signposted to the west to Kinnordy. Immediately after this is another minor road signposted Kinwhirrie and this is your route.

After about 2 miles you will reach a ford which unlike many other fords, is a) normally full of water and b) more than occasionally impassable for the average cyclist. However there is a small footbridge just upstream. Soon after the ford, the road meets a T junction where you turn left along an up and down road till another T junction where you go right to Balintore. The road now runs along the side of Cat Law, an outlier of the Grampian Mountains. Eventually, after a number of significant ups and downs, the semi-ruin of Balintore Castle appears on your right. Go up to the castle if you have time. It is a Victorian building which is currently undergoing long term restoration. The view from the castle is one of the finest in this part of Scotland.

Balintore Castle

After a final small hill at Balintore, the road bears sharply to the left and after a couple of miles, you reach Pitmudie and the shores of Loch of Lintrathen. At the crossroads you can go straight across and along the north west side of the loch or turn left along the north east and south east sides. (If you are really keen you could turn right and head up Glen Isla, reversing the direction of Route 13 but that would make this a significantly longer route than anything else in this book.) Whichever way you go, apart from right, you will end up at the south west corner of the loch, ready to carry on along Route 14 and home to Coupar Angus.

The Coupar Angus cycle purist might want to start this route and Route 14 for that matter, differently, by going up the A923 on the route to Blairgowrie then turning right after the Couttie Bridge over the Isla and, ultimately, back over the Isla at Kitty Swanson's Bridge. Whilst technically a more pure route, as you could stay completely within the boundaries of the Blairgowrie and Forfar roads, it is not recommended because of the relatively slow start.

The Castle 20 minutes later

Lintrathen again

Ice Cream in Kirriemuir

To be honest, Route 16 is a bit of a mongrel. It is the only route in this book which is almost completely on other routes though there is a small bit that is unique. One of the beauties of the ride is, however, that it gives you time to look around the interesting town of Kirriemuir. Kirrie, as it is known locally, also features in Route 15 but on that route you will probably be in a hurry to get along to the ford and Balintore Castle so might not spend much time in the town.

So, follow Route 15 all the way to the centre of Kirrie where, it is recommended, you stop in one of its many tearooms. Have a look at the Peter Pan statue in the town centre, go along to J.M.Barrie's birthplace (very well signed, you cannot miss it) then head off for the Camera Obscura on the north side of Kirrie for some great views of the Angus and Perthshire countryside. Two other features of Kirrie worth mentioning are 1) Visocchi's ice cream parlour and 2) it is also the birthplace of Sir Hugh Munro who catalogued all those 3000ft Scottish mountains.

Route 16 leaves Kirriemuir on the B951 to Kirkton of Kingoldrum – impressive name, not sure the village lives up to it. To find this road from the centre of Kirrie, start on the Glens Road but then head off to the west. Carry on along the B961 till you get to the turn off for Bridgend of Lintrathen (about 2.5 miles) where you turn left to reach the village and, immediately after, the shore of Loch of Lintrathen. There are two ways home to Coupar Angus from here. First you could stay beside the loch until you get to its south west corner and then follow the route back to base as described in To the Lovely Loch of Lintrathen. Alternatively find the spot where the road from Ruthven meets the loch, as described in the start of route 14 and reverse the route from here back to Coupar Angus. This junction is just over a bridge as you come out of Bridgend of Lintrathen and to the left. Either route back is interesting.

Ruthven Church

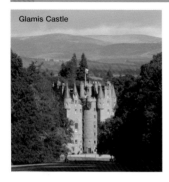

Glamis Castle

The area around Coupar Angus is rich with antiquities, notably standing stones both out in the field and indoors. The Stones Tour majors on some of the best examples of Pictish stones in the area to the east of Coupar Angus. The tour also touches on the village of Glamis and a visit to the romantic Glamis Castle with its fond family connections to the late Queen Elizabeth the Queen Mother and the late Princess Margaret's birthplace, is a must. Most of the tour is in the very heart of Strathmore and the views are outstanding. As you approach Glamis, you will move from the county of Perthshire into the adjoining county of Angus.

Leave the Y Café in Coupar Angus and head for the A94 to Forfar. After 200 yards, turn right onto the minor road to Meigle via Ardler. This is a pretty road which runs parallel to the A94 and is very quiet apart, in the summer and early spring, from the necessary tractors. When you arrive in Meigle turn into the village and there is a fascinating museum of Pictish stones on the other side of the road. (There is a detour you can do before Meigle to look at the 'High Keillor' Standing Stone, if you look at the map the stone is marked on it.)

Eassie Churchyard

Leave Meigle on the road to Dundee and turn left to Kirkinch after about half a mile. Follow the minor road to a T junction and turn right into Kirkinch village. Go through the village and at the next T junction turn left to Kirkton of Nevay, Balkeerie, Eassie and the A94 at Glamis. Great views all the way along this road of the mountains on the other side of Strathmore. Cross the A94 and go into the village. Glamis Castle and Angus Folk Museum are worth a visit to show two totally different aspects of life in Angus. Look out for a Pictish stone in the manse garden. This is one of the best preserved stones which is still outdoors.

The Eassie Pictish Stone

Start the return journey the way you came, back along the road to Eassie taking the first proper road on the right down to the A94. Turn right to Eassie Farm and the ruined church (with sensitively enclosed Pictish Stone). If you have space on your bike, and somewhere to cook it, make sure you buy some home grown asparagus from Eassie Farm. Back onto the A94 towards Meigle and Coupar Angus, turn right after less than 100 yards and follow signs to Craigton.

Cross the Dean Water, great views of Strathmore in all directions. After about 1 mile turn left on the road to Cardean and Meigle. Look out for the Ospreys' nest on top of the pylon where the two electricity power lines in this area meet. At the end of this minor road turn left onto the B954 and then immediately left onto the A94 and back to Meigle. In the centre of Meigle turn right and then right again onto the minor road to Ardler and thence follow the route back to Coupar Angus.

For refreshments there are tearooms and a pub in Ardler, Meigle (perhaps just for the return route or the far point may never be reached) and Glamis (the far point). The total route is about 30 miles and takes between 3 and 6 hours depending on how many stops. This route stays in the Vale of Strathmore and, while there are ups and downs, there are no steep hills.

Route 18 is quite short and mostly flat but it still manages to find some interesting places to visit. We start by leaving Coupar Angus by exit 6, the route that goes over Kitty Swanson's Bridge. So start off up the A923 out of Coupar Angus towards Blairgowrie. Unfortunately there is no alternative to this at the moment though there is pressure to use the remains of the rail bridge, you will see this just to the west of the road bridge over the Isla, as the basis of a cycle route. For the moment, just take care as you ride along the A923, particularly as you cross Couttie Bridge.

The Bendochy Swap Shop

For the first part of this route you are following Route 1 in this book, 'Le Tour de Coupar Angus'. If you refer to Route 1 you will see that your tour turns right off the Blairgowrie road, along towards Ryehill and then along the Ericht Path and over Kitty Swanson's Bridge. Kitty Swanson operated a ferry across the River Ericht at this point for many years back in the 1800s, so the bridge replaced her ferry! It was nice of the builders to remember the now, presumably redundant, Kitty by naming the bridge after her. Assuming she was still alive when the bridge opened, I hope the builders gave her a pension.

Meigle Pictish Stones

Still following Route 1, after the bridge, instead of turning right to the Metal Bridge over the Isla, keep straight on until you meet a T junction with the B954. Here you turn right for Meigle with its interesting Pictish Stones Museum. Leaving Meigle on the B954 to Newtyle and Dundee, within 3 miles you will arrive at Newtyle. Turn right in the centre and left off the larger minor road onto a very minor road that climbs up to Leys just before the main A923 Coupar Angus to Dundee road. Beautiful views to the north all the way along this road, across the Vale of Strathmore towards the Grampians.

Kilpurnie Hill above Newtyle

Cross over the A923 and make a right turn at the first crossroad down into Campmuir. Turn right in Campmuir and you are soon back in Coupar Angus.

A short ride but with refreshments in Meigle, at the Belmont Arms (formerly The Junction) and in Newtyle itself. There are opportunities to cycle parts of the Newtyle to Coupar Angus railway line; you will pass it at a couple of points, but it does not look as if the complete route will be available, at least not in the short to medium term.

A lovely trip into another one of the beautiful hanging valleys in the Sidlaws. Though you pass over the Sidlaw watershed twice, there are no steep hills on this route, just lochs, rolling hills, views of the mountains and mostly very peaceful roads.

Leave Coupar Angus beside Larghan Park and head for Ardler and Meigle as in 'The Stones Tour'. When you get to Meigle you turn right onto the B954 direction Newtyle and Dundee. You will see lots of evidence of old railway lines around here and just before you enter Newtyle, you will pass a disused railway bridge. As mentioned in route 18, some of the old railway lines have been converted into paths which can be cycled. But since the roads are mostly very quiet, there is little advantage to these paths. Pass through Newtyle and start up the gentle gradient into the Sidlaws. To your right you will see the old Dundee to Newtyle railway and, as this indicates, the climb is never steep.

Hatton Castle, Newtyle

Lundie Bus Shelter

Just over the summit at 161 metres you come to one of the smallest, and smartest, bus shelters in Perthshire and this is the signal to leave the B954 by turning right and following the sign to Lundie. After a short climb you are in a very fertile valley which leads to Thriepley, look out for the large house on the right with its Italian garden and very ornate summer house.

Past the house there is a loch and if you turn right at the end of the loch you can cycle up to Wester Keith and a really peaceful fishing loch. Unfortunately the road is a dead end and you need to return to the 'main' road by the loch. Turn right and carry on till a T junction where you turn right again, pass through Lundie and hit the main Dundee to Coupar Angus road (A923) half a mile short of its summit. Turn right onto the main road till you reach a car park where the view to the north opens up. This is Tullybaccart and, if you are lucky, there may be a coffee van parked here owned by the local Stark family. It is cheekily called Starkbucks!

The Italian Summer House

There are three routes back to Coupar Angus from here. The simples one is to stay on the A923 and just go down the hill to your starting point. Route two is a little more complex. Follow the sign at Tullybaccart to the Laird's Loch (on the west side of the road). Go along the north side of the loch, past its end and you come to a T junction. This last bit may be difficult to cycle. At the T turn left on to a good track which snakes around Northballo Hill till you get to the minor road from Coupar Angus to Abernyte. Turn right on to the road and very soon you will be shooting down a steep hill which, if you stay on this road, will take you into the village of Campmuir where you turn right and back into Coupar Angus.

Finally, and for a more sporting route, turn left just before Tullybaccart onto the minor road to East Newton. Take the first proper road to your right (2 miles) and at a T junction which soon appears, turn right again. Now you have to climb up the main hill on the Abernyte to Coupar Angus road. Eventually, as in Route 2, you will find yourself in Campmuir and here you turn right again for Coupar Angus. See also Route 2 (Over the Sidlaws) for more details of the routes home.

HMF Unicorn (by Sandy Roberston, GSR Photographic)

Route 20 is, I am ashamed to say, a bit of a fraud. It is really just a very interesting cycle around Dundee but, since you can easily cycle from Coupar Angus to Dundee, or, if necessary, sling your bike on the back of a car, it seems okay to include the route in this book. The circular route around Dundee is really quite complex, is well described both in a pamphlet which can be obtained from the city council and online, and is well signed. For these reasons it is not intended to describe 'Le Tour de Dundee' in great detail in this book. Rather you will be guided onto the route, given information of how to access details of the route and then left to your own devices.

So, starting in Coupar Angus, the first objective is to get to Camperdown Park in Dundee. Take the A923 south out of Coupar Angus and enter the park just south of Muirhead via the first roundabout that you come to, just before Dundee's ringroad, the Kingsway. Turn right at the roundabout and then right again into the park. Go up to Camperdown House and you will see signs for the 'Dundee Green Circular', the route around Dundee. Getting from Coupar Angus to Dundee really means using the main road.

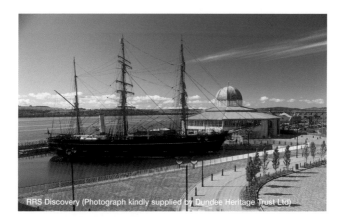
RRS Discovery (Photograph kindly supplied by Dundee Heritage Trust Ltd)

A couple of websites provide a map and details of Dundee's Green Circular, for example:

http://www.dundeetravelinfo.com/downloads/Dundee%20Cycle%20Map%202012.pdf

http://visuals.sdgworld.net/temp/dundeetravelactive/downloads/gcroute.pdf

Also copies of the map are available in the main Dundee Library, the Dundee Travel Active shop in the Wellgate and the Tourist Information Point at Discovery Point in Dundee.

If you start in Camperdown Park and follow the signs in an easterly direction, you will pass through Templeton Woods, Clatto, Den O'Mains and Trottick Ponds Nature areas, the Dighty Water, Finlathen Park, Drumgeith Meadow, Claypotts Castle, Broughty Ferry Castle, beach, harbour, and beautiful Rock Garden, Customs House, the Frigate Unicorn, Discovery Point, the Esplanade, the Tay Road and Rail Bridges then back up to Camperdown Park. The route is around 26 miles and full of interest. Though the signage is normally very good, having the Dundee City Council Cycle map in your back pocket would be very useful. At the time of writing, cycling through the Dundee Port area requires some documentation and I recommend you check the City Council website before setting off on 'Le Tour de Dundee'.

Coupar Angus to Camperdown is about 10 miles, so the whole trip on a bike would be 46 miles. Though there are ways of avoiding the main A923 from Coupar Angus to Dundee, they tend to be fairly long and arduous, for example the climb over the Sidlaws from Campmuir to Abernyte, and cannot really be recommended.

Route 21 is long, make no mistake about it. The route starts in Eastern
Perthshire, goes through Angus then into the Mearns. The Mearns is
Aberdeenshire and is rich, big, farming land with wide open spaces backed
by the Grampian Mountains. The route follows the foot of the mountains and
there are no hard climbs, but it is a long way. In addition, unless you have
friends/relations who will pick you up, you will need to take your bike on the
train back from Stonehaven, where the route finishes, to Dundee. And then
cycle the 12 or so miles from Dundee to Coupar Angus (see Route 20). Before
you leave, check the train times from Laurencekirk to Dundee, you will see why
later. Finally, the map in this guide does not stretch all the way to Stonehaven,
so an OS map or two might be necessary. Altogether an interesting but
long trip.

Leave Coupar Angus by the back road to Meigle (see Stones Tour). From
Meigle take the minor road towards Kirriemuir (see Route 15). Eventually you
will reach the A928 Dundee to Kirriemuir Road, cross straight over on a minor
road which joins the A926 (Forfar to Kirriemuir) just before Padanaram (Paddie
to the locals). Turn right towards Forfar and cycle into the town. Forfar is complex
as far as roads are concerned, but well signed. You are looking for the B9134
to Brechin (initially you may follow signs for the A932 to Arbroath) but, at a
complex junction on the east side of Forfar, the B9134 will appear. And now the
route is straightforward for a while. Up and down minor hills and along to meet
the A935 just before Brechin. Turn right and, at Brechin Castle, right again and
into the town. (Forget it if you are trying to use OS maps at this point.

Edzell Arch

Brechin is on the edge of about 4 of them!) In Brechin follow the signs out of the town towards the A90 and Aberdeen. Just before you reach the main road there is a roundabout, an underpass and signs for Edzell. This is your route. Things are simpler for a while. The minor road you are on enters Edzell through an arch (there are lots of them around here, built in honour of Queen Victoria who liked the area).

The Grand Fettercairn Arch

Leaving Edzell on the same road you soon cross the River North Esk (interesting falls on your left if you have time to explore) and the road carries on to Fettercairn (another triumphal arch and a distillery). Now you have a chance to bail out, but only if you have checked the train times from Laurencekirk. It is about 4 miles on the B9120 (flat or downhill) from Fettercairn to Laurencekirk and this will save you the last 20 miles or so.

Assuming you are carrying on, be sure NOT to get onto the B974 road out of Fettercairn. A lovely road with some very gorgeous hills. You want the B966 which you stay on until you see signs for Auchenblae. Turn left for this pretty little village. Auchenblae is a bit of a maze of roads and you are looking for a very minor, minor road which leaves the village in a north westerly direction and then snakes around though Glenfarquhar, Dillavaird, Inchbreck, Elfhill and Tewel until eventually you reach the A90 Forfar to Aberdeen road. Cross over the main road on a flyover and follow the signs for Stonehaven Station. About 60 miles all told.

Now you catch the train back to Dundee and follow the road signs from Dundee Station to Coupar Angus. You will be on the A923, a significant, for these parts, commuter road. However fairly quiet before 4.30 and after 6.30 pm.

As it says at the start, Route 21 is a very long but very interesting tour.

The SHORT TOURS

The routes in this section do not, in general, take you onto new roads, they are on old favourites but with one or two new links. Try these routes if you are wanting to sample the area but, perhaps avoid Route 22 which includes a steep climb over the Sidlaws.

22 Abernyte Tour · 20 miles : 2.5 hours

Using roads that make up part of the Macbeth's Castle and Dunsinane Hill tour, Route 22 leaves Coupar Angus on the road to Campmuir. In Campmuir turn left and take the third turning on the right that you come to, signposted Collace and Kinrossie. In the centre of Collace turn left up the side of Dunsinane Hill and turn left onto the B953 to Abernyte. There are steep hills around here as you cross the backbone of the Sidlaw Hills.

The road goes into Abernyte and follows down to a large antique show room containing a small tearoom/restaurant – the Scottish Antique and Arts Centre. Beware here because you are going to have to retrace your steps after visiting the centre so, if the hill looks scary, then don't go down it but rather go back to the fork in the road just above Abernyte. To the left is the road you have just come along, from Dunsinane, to the right is a small road which will take you back to Campmuir.

Turn right then take the first left along the west side of Northballo Hill and down the very steep hill to Campmuir. Turn right in Campmuir and back to Coupar Angus.

A very short ride but not one to do as a first outing. There is very little flat riding and the climbing is long and arduous (or exhilarating and challenging if you are sufficiently fit).

Towards the Sidlaws

A short, mostly flattish route and a good introduction to the start of some of the tours on the south side of the A94 Perth to Forfar road.

Leave Coupar Angus on the Campmuir Road but turn left after half a mile. Ignoring a left turn to Kettins, continue along this road till a crossroad where you turn left. Soon you reach the main A923 which you cross and climb a short hill to Leys. After about 1 mile, a farm road leads down the face of the hill (not as steep as this sounds) to Halliburton House. Keep going north on this road, past the house till you meet a T junction. I have never seen this farm road closed but your alternatives are to a) retrace your route back to Coupar Angus, b) carry on along the road through Leys till you hit the Newtyle to Coupar Angus road, where you turn left back to Coupar Angus, or c) go back to the A923 and turn right for Coupar Angus.

However, assuming that the farm road IS open, and that you have reached the T junction, turn left and soon you will be in the hamlet of Kettins. Keep on the same road and you will reach the A923. Cross the main road and at the T junction you passed at the start of the route, turn right and back into Coupar Angus.

This very short route is flat as it just follows the Vale of Strathmore to the east and then returns. No new ground here and most of the roads described have been covered before, but not all!

Leave Coupar Angus on the A94 towards Forfar and before Larghan Park, turn right past 'East of Scotland Farmers'. You are now on the road to Meigle. Cross the long defunct Coupar Angus to Forfar railway line and at the first T junction turn left. And cycle to Meigle, it is about 4 miles. Stop in Meigle for tearooms, pub and/or Pictish stones, then take the B954 to Newtyle and Dundee.

Meigle Stones

Just to the south of Meigle the road goes round a couple of bends to the right then the left, then straightens up again. You will soon come to a track where you turn right. This track brings you back onto the road to Coupar Angus so just retrace your steps (pedals) back to your starting point.

This is the easiest route in the book. If, as you are leaving Meigle you feel up to a bigger challenge, then look out for Routes 18, 19 or, even, 17. If not, then just enjoy the peaceful roads and the tranquil beauty of the Vale of Strathmore.

This route is simply the first part of 'Le Tour de Coupar Angus'. It would be great to be able to say that there are absolutely no hills. Unfortunately this is not true as the route crosses the Ericht and the Isla and then 'climbs' back out of the flood plain of these two rivers and up to the villages on the north side of the Sidlaws. But using the word climb is a bit misleading and the hill you go up is really just a gentle incline. Of course you could reverse the route and the gentle incline becomes a great downhill. However the route then has a short sting in its tail, the climb from the Couttie Bridge over the Isla back up to Coupar Angus. The choice is yours!

The River Isla (Photograph JR)

So leave Coupar Angus on the A923 Blairgowrie Road and follow Routes 1 and 18 around to Kitty Swanson's Bridge. After the bridge you follow route 1 and cross the rather attractive metal bridge over the River Isla. Now comes the 'hill' up to the A94. If this hill bothers you, don't worry. After a few more of the routes in this book, you will no longer notice it at all. Turn left, very briefly, onto the A923 then right to the small village of Ardler – complete with its attractive pub.

Turn right in Ardler and follow the road back to Coupar Angus; you will need to make a right turn after about 1.5 miles to bring you back to Larghan Park.

The last route in the book and a bit of an odd one. Indeed a recent trip suggested that reaching the gull colony in Route 26 is now almost impossible due to fallen trees and waterlogging. However, if we ever get back to good old fashioned east of Scotland dry summers then the last bit of the route will be possible again.

Leave Coupar Angus by the A923 and this time you have to stay on the road for a bit longer. Go straight over the crossroads where you would turn right for Kitty Swanson's Bridge and up the hill towards Blairgowrie. A few hundred yards after the top of the hill, Myreriggs Road goes off to the right. You need to turn left at this point and onto a farm track past Stormont Loch, a Site of Special Scientific Interest. Indeed the whole of this area is a nature reserve.

Stormont Loch

Stormont Loch

Carry on to the end of the loch to a farm where you bear right, through a gate and into the forest. This is where the path becomes difficult and may even be impassable. You soon come to a second loch, Hare Myre Loch and this is where the gull colony is hidden. Normally it is just about possible to walk around the loch but on a recent visit, flooding made this impossible. However, if you can make it, the gull colony is in the north west corner of the loch and is quite a sight, and quite a sound.

Returning to Stormont Loch, a site for outdoor curling as recently as 2011/12, go back down to the main A923. You have two choices now, turn right back along the main road or go straight across the main road to Myreriggs Road and enter the network of minor roads which will eventually bring you back onto the A923 just before Couttie Bridge.

Winter Fun on Stormont Loch

If you opt for the latter, follow the road as far to the east as it goes, near Ryehill, then bear right onto the road to Kitty Swanson's Bridge. You will soon be back on the A923 and then you have no choice - the Couttie Bridge and the A923 or nothing.

Tearooms and Sources of Refreshment on the Cycle Routes

This list of cafes, restaurants and inns is by no means exhaustive. Rather it is designed to point cyclists in the direction of places where they can get drinks, light meals etc., particularly in the more remote destinations. For more information on selected tearooms in Strathmore, a recommended read is 'Tearoom Delights: a little guide to delightful tearooms of Perthshire, Angus and Dundee' by Lorna McInnes (**www.teacupspress.com**). Readers can check nearly all the establishments on Google. Most of the out of the way inns are very happy to provide teas, coffees and light lunches to cyclists. If in doubt, just contact them before you set off. Where addresses of tearooms are not given, it is because the villages they are in are so small that finding them is not a problem. I must admit that I have not visited every single establishment listed so their appearance on the list is not a recommendation. Mind you, nearly all the ones I have visited are excellent. Finally, some towns and villages have so many places to eat and drink that individual listings are not necessary.

Coupar Angus

- Red House Hotel, open every day for tea, coffee, meals, etc
  Accommodation available, parking for cars and a fitness centre
  01828 628500 or www.red-house-hotel.co.uk

- Café Isla Community Café, Union Street, Coupar Angus
  Open Wednesdays, Thursday and Fridays from 11-3pm for drinks, light lunches, snacks, etc

- Tower Café, High Street, Coupar Angus
  Open from early morning to 4pm every day except Sunday for drinks and light snacks

Abernyte

- Scottish Antique and Arts Centre, restaurant and food centre
  Open 7 days a week from 10 till 4pm
  01828 686401 or www.scottish-antiques.com

Balbeggie

- Macdonald Arms Hotel, Main Street, Balbeggie for drink, lunches, dinners and accommodation
  01821 640242 or www.macdonaldarmshotel.com

Burrelton

- Burrelton Park Hotel, High Street, Burrelton
  Drinks, meals and accommodation
  01828 670206 or www.burreltonpark.co.uk

Stanley

- The Apron Stage for lunch (Friday) or evening meals
  Small, French type restaurant
  01738 828888 or www.apronstagerestaurant.co.uk

- Tayside Hotel, Mill Street, Stanley for drinks, lunches, dinner
  and accommodation
  01738 828249 or www.taysidehotel.co.uk

Bankfoot

- Stewart Tower Dairy, near Stanley for drinks and light meals and
  in particular, wonderful homemade Italian gelato-style ice cream in
  almost 200 flavours
  01738 710044 or www.stewart-tower.co.uk
  Open 7 days a week from 10-4.30

Meikleour

- Meikleour Hotel and Inn for drinks, snacks, meals and accommodation
  01250 883206 or www.meikleourhotel.co.uk

Dunkeld and Birnam

- These linked towns are full of hotels, tearooms and pubs and also the
  excellent Birnam Institute. The cyclist is well catered for here and there
  is a cycle shop - Progression Bikes, Dunkeld
  07825 322 225 www.progressionbikesscotland.com

Murthly

- No eateries or drinkeries in Murthly but there is a shop/garage if you have
  run out of supplies on that 'once in a life-time' scorching hot summer's day

Butterstone

- Butterstone Loch Bistro and Café just off the A923 from Blairgowrie
  to Dunkeld. For drinks, lunches or an evening meal right next to the
  lovely Butterstone Loch
  01350 724238 or www.butterstonelochfishings.cu.uk

Pitlochry

- A major tourist town on the main A9 to the Highlands. Full of restaurants, tearooms, pubs and inns

Ballinluig

- Ballinluig Motor Grill – not really designed for cyclists but if you are stuck for something to eat and drink on the Pitlochry cycle (Route 10) then the BMG might just rescue you. Open 8am - 8.30pm every day

Kirkmichael

- Kirkmichael Hotel – a small coaching Inn with bar in the village of Kirkmichael. 01250 881769 or www.kirkmichaelhotel.co.uk

- The Strathardle Inn, just east of Kirkmichael, for bar, meals and accommodation. 01250 881224 or www.strathardleinn.co.uk

Bridge of Cally

- Bridge of Cally Hotel, right in the centre of this tiny village, for drinks, light meals, dinner, accommodation, etc 01250 886231 or www.bridgeofcallyhotel.com

Blairgowrie

- Known to its inhabitants as 'Blair' - a largish town with a number of good tearooms, restaurants and inns plus a cycle shop (Crighton's Cycles, 87 Perth Street, Blairgowrie) 01250 710852 or http://www.crightonscyclesperthshire.co.uk/

Kirkton of Glenisla

- Kirkton of Glenisla Hotel, on the B951 a long way from anywhere (apart from Kirkton of Glenisla of course) for drinks, light meals, dinner, accommodation, access to cycle trails, etc 01575 582223 or www.glenisla-hotel.com

Loch of Lintrathen

- Peel Farm Tearoom, near the south west corner of the Loch of Lintrathen, for drinks and light meals and lots more including an extensive farm shop and craft shop. 01575 660205 or www.peelfarm.com Open every day throughout the year

Alyth

- Singing Kettle, 14 Airlie Street
  Victorian style café with excellent cakes from 'Cakes by Sally'
  01828 632426 or www.cakesbysally.co.uk/The_Singing_Kettle.htm

- The Dirliebane, 2 Market Square for drinks and light meals
  01828 633644

Kirriemuir

- Kirriemuir has a number of tearooms, restaurants and inns

Meigle

- The Joinery Café for drinks and light lunches
  Open 7 days a week in the summer, closed Tuesdays in the winter
  01828 640717 or www.meiglecoffeeshop.co.uk

- Cardeans Bistro for light lunches, snacks and home baking throughout the
  week except Monday
  01828 640740 or www.cardeans.com

- Belmont Arms Hotel is a mile south of Meigle on the road to Newtyle
  Drinks, snacks, meals and accommodation
  01828 640232 or www.belmontarms.co.uk

- The Kinloch Arms Hotel, The Square
  Drinks, snacks, meals and accommodation
  01828 640251

Glamis

- The Victorian Tearoom at Glamis Castle for drinks, meals and home baking
  Open 29th March to 31st December
  0845 0267915 or www.glamis-castle.co.uk/tour-restaurants.cfm

- The Strathmore Arms, 1 The Square, for drinks, light lunches, meals
  and accommodation. 01307 840248 or www.strathmorearmsglamis.com

Newtyle

- Commercial Hotel, South Street. Drinks and snacks
  01828 650469

Ardler

- The Tavern, traditional village pub in the centre of Ardler
  Opening hours susceptible to change

Family Cycles in the Vale of Strathmore

Most, but not all, of the cycles in 'Adventures on Two Wheels ...' are on minor roads. Family Cycles in the Vale of Strathmore will report only on routes that use minor roads. The routes will be relatively short, mostly between 5 and 15 miles, and all will be suitable for families, with minor roads, tearooms, places and sights of interest. Watch out for Family Cycles around the end of 2013.

Off Road in Eastern Perthshire

Perthshire abounds in fabulous off road routes, many of them centring around the Tay Valley and the A9. Eastern Perthshire, the land to the east of the Tay, is less well explored though its potential is as big, if not more, than other regions of the county. In 'Off Road in Eastern Perthshire' the author will explore the off road equivalent of 'Adventures on Two Wheels ...'.

With these two books, and the current one that you are reading, the reader will have a very comprehensive guide to all the best cycle routes in Eastern Perthshire, from the Sidlaw Hills in the south to the Grampians in the north and, in between of course, the beautiful Vale of Strathmore.

West Strathmore

On retiring from his post as head of science at a Scottish University, John Palfreyman decided to combine his love of Scotland, in particular the Vale of Strathmore, and his love of cycling, to produce this guide book. John has been cycling the byways of this particularly beautiful but largely unknown, except by its grateful inhabitants, area of Scotland for the last 30 years and is always amazed at the new routes, vistas, tearooms, and inns that can be discovered along the hidden roads of Strathmore.

A field of flax near Ardler

How to use the Map

Attached to the back cover of this book is a detailed map of the central part of the Vale of Strathmore and the surrounding hills and mountains. Most of the 26 routes described in 'Adventures on Two Wheels ...' are detailed on this map though it does not include the northern most part of Route 10 ('Via Kirkmichael to Pitlochry'), the eastern most parts of Route 21 ('Through Angus and the Mearns'), or the Dundee bit of Route 20 which can be found at the website mentioned in the text.

Each route in the book is indicated on the map by a different colour and/or type of line. However, and to avoid confusion, where various use the same road (for example the road from Coupar Angus to Meigle features regularly in the text) then just one line is drawn.

Your 'Adventures on Two Wheels ...' map includes aspects of OS maps 43, 44, 45, 53 and 54, though all of the shorter routes are on Landranger Map 53 – Blairgowrie and surrounding area. If you lose the map in this book, further copies can be ordered from the author at a cost of £3.99.

Strathmore Harvest